OCR
TEXT PROCESSING
(BUSINESS PROFESSIONAL)

LEVEL 1 BOOK **1**

Official Publisher Partnership

OCR
TEXT PROCESSING
(BUSINESS PROFESSIONAL)
LEVEL 1 BOOK 1

TEXT PRODUCTION, WORD PROCESSING
AND AUDIO TRANSCRIPTION

EDITOR: JILL DOWSON

ROSALIND BUXTON • LESLEY DAKIN • SYLVIA ELKINS
• BEVERLY LORAM • JANE QUIBELL • JEAN RAY • PAM SMITH

AN HACHETTE UK COMPANY

Orders: please contact Bookpoint Ltd, 130 Milton Park, Abingdon, Oxon OX14 4SB.
Telephone: +44 (0)1235 827720. Fax: +44 (0)1235 400454. Lines are open from 9.00am to 5.00pm,
Monday to Saturday, with a 24-hour message-answering service. You can also order through our website
www.hoddereducation.co.uk

If you have any comments to make about this, or any of our other titles, please send them to
educationenquiries@hodder.co.uk

British Library Cataloguing in Publication Data
A catalogue record for this title is available from the British Library

ISBN: 978 1 444 10789 0

First Edition Published 2010
Impression number   10 9 8 7 6 5 4 3 2 1
Year   2013 2012 2011 2010

Hachette UK's policy is to use papers that are natural, renewable and recyclable products and made from
wood grown in sustainable forests. The logging and manufacturing processes are expected to conform to
the environmental regulations of the country of origin.

Cover photo © Influx Productions
Typeset by Dorchester Typesetting Group Ltd
Printed in Malta for Hodder Education, an Hachette UK company, 338 Euston Road, London NW1 3BH

CONTENTS

THE AUTHORS

The following authors, who have provided all the material for this book, are Chief Examiners/Examiners for the Oxford, Cambridge and RSA Examination Board: Rosalind Buxton, Lesley Dakin, Sylvia Elkins, Beverly Loram, Jane Quibell, Jean Ray and Pam Smith. The Series Editor is Jill Dowson.

STUDENT TEXTBOOKS IN THE TEXT PROCESSING (BUSINESS PROFESSIONAL) SUITE PUBLISHED BY HODDER EDUCATION, ENDORSED BY OCR EXAMINATION BOARD

Level 1 – Book 1 Text Production – core unit Word Processing Audio-Transcription	Level 1 – Book 2 Mailmerge Business Presentations Legal Text Processing
Level 2 – Book 1* Text Production – core unit Word Processing Audio-Transcription	Level 2 – Book 2 Medical Word Processing Medical Audio-Transcription Legal Audio-Transcription
Level 2 – Book 3 Mailmerge Business Presentations Document Presentation	
Level 3 – Book 1 Text Production – core unit Word Processing Audio-Transcription	Level 3 – Book 2 Legal Word Processing Document Presentation

* Level 2 – Book 1 is available to order from the Hodder Education website (www.hoddereducation.co.uk). Level 3 – Book 1 will be published early in 2010. Material covering the other units is also planned for 2010.

1 | INTRODUCTION

About the book

This series of textbooks is designed for you to build on the knowledge and skills you have already acquired so that you can progress to more advanced and varied text processing work in order to gain an Award, Certificate and Diploma in Text Processing (Business Professional).

It presumes that you already have a basic knowledge of the keyboard and how to use Microsoft® Word, or similar software, to produce basic documents.

This book contains the background information, practice exercises and practice exams you require to prepare for the OCR Text Processing (Business Professional) exam units in:

- Text Production Level 1
- Word Processing Level 1
- Audio-Transcription Level 1.

The book is divided into the following sections.

- **Introduction:** this covers the contents of the book, together with an overview of the Text Processing (Business Professional) suite of qualifications at Level 1.
- **Assessment Criteria:** this section contains the syllabuses, or unit content at the time of going to press, for the three units. Each syllabus lists the items you will be tested on in the exams, and the relevant knowledge, understanding and skills that you need to acquire in order to complete these exams. It also gives details of the marking schemes, complete with tutors' notes, so that you can see exactly how your exam paper will be marked. Visit the Text Processing pages on the OCR website for any unit updates at www.ocr.org.uk.
- **Knowledge, Understanding and Skills:** this section provides detailed notes together with exercises that enable you to practise the skills you need to master before attempting a full practice exam for each unit. Following each set of notes, there are three examples of each type of document. Templates, recall text, graphics and dictation are available on the Hodder Plus website at **www.hodderplus.co.uk/ocrtextprocessing**.
- **Exam work:** this section provides hints for exam work, together with three new practice exams similar to the OCR standard for each unit. Templates, recall text, graphics and dictation are available on the Hodder Plus website at **www.hodderplus.co.uk/ocrtextprocessing**.
- **Worked examples:** correct worked examples of all practice exercises and exams are supplied in this section. Note that each of these shows only one

way of displaying the documents – for example, your method of emphasis may not be the same, your line ends may differ slightly or you may have left extra linespacing after headings. This is acceptable, as long as you have followed instructions and formatted your document consistently.

The Text Processing (Business Professional) suite of qualifications

Overview of Level 1

The Text Processing suite of qualifications has been designed to develop and recognise candidates' ability to produce a variety of current and straightforward business documents to meet the requirements of the employer in a modern business environment. The units that make up these qualifications have been developed from the RSA Text Processing Modular Awards Stage I, which have been widely recognised by employers as benchmark qualifications in text processing. The qualifications are nationally accredited on to the Qualifications & Credit Framework (QCF).

The qualifications at Level 1 are suitable for candidates who:

• are new to the skills and knowledge required by text processing operators
• are studying in preparation for employment.

Qualification structures

Candidates enter each unit separately and a unit certificate will be issued. On achievement of each unit the candidate will be awarded a number of credits. If a candidate wishes to achieve a Text Processing (Business Professional) Award, Certificate or Diploma, credits will need to be accumulated as described in the boxes below.

OCR Text Processing (Business Professional) Level 1 Award – 06947 (English)/04607 (Welsh)

The full OCR Level 1 Award in Text Processing (Business Professional) is awarded when the candidate has successfully completed **units to the value of at least eight credits**.

- Four of these credits must come from a Level 1 core unit: Text Production, Cynhyrchu Testun (Welsh) or Text Production – Screen Reader. The assessment criteria is almost identical for each version of the core unit, therefore candidates may choose only one.
- The remaining four credits can be taken from the Level 1 or 2 optional units listed in OCR's Centre Handbook.
- In order to receive the Welsh Award (Dyfarniad Lefel 1), a candidate should be entered for the core unit (03945) and either 03946 or 03948 as their optional unit.

Please note that some combinations of units are barred – for full details of rules of combination candidates should refer to their centres or access the OCR website on www.ocr.org.uk

OCR Text Processing (Business Professional) Level 1 Certificate – 06948

The full OCR Level 1 Certificate in Text Processing (Business Professional) is awarded when the candidate has successfully completed **units to the value of at least 13 credits**.

- Four of these credits must come from a Level 1 core unit, Text Production, Cynhyrchu Testun (Welsh) or Text Production – Screen Reader. The assessment criteria is almost identical for each version of the core unit, therefore candidates may choose only one.
- Of the remaining credits, a minimum of four must be taken from the Level 1 or 2 optional units listed in OCR's Centre Handbook.
- Further credits required may be taken from Entry Level Speed Keying.

Please note that some combinations of units are barred – for full details of rules of combination candidates should refer to their centres or access the OCR website on www.ocr.org.uk

---

OCR Text Processing (Business Professional) Level 1 Diploma – 06949

The full OCR Level 1 Diploma in Text Processing (Business Professional) is awarded when the candidate has successfully completed **units to the value of at least 37 credits**.

- Four of these credits must come from a Level 1 core unit, Text Production, Cynhyrchu Testun (Welsh) or Text Production – Screen Reader. The assessment criteria is almost identical for each version of the core unit, therefore candidates may choose only one.
- Of the remaining credits, a minimum of 19 must be taken from the Level 1 or 2 optional units listed in OCR's Centre Handbook.
- Further credits required may be taken from Entry Level Speed Keying.

Please note that some combinations of units are barred – for full details of rules of combination candidates should refer to their centres or access the OCR website on www.ocr.org.uk

---

The credits attached to the units achieved within each qualification are banked and may then contribute to the next qualification at the same level (eg if a candidate has achieved the required credit for the Level 2 Award, this credit can also be carried forward to the Level 1 Certificate).

Due to the flexible nature of qualifications within the QCF, these banked credits may also contribute to a higher qualification at a later stage of the candidate's progress.

Form of assessment

Each unit within the qualifications is assessed via an OCR-set and marked examination.

Candidates will be required to carry out all assessment tasks within a stated error tolerance.

Results will be graded Distinction, Pass or Fail, depending upon the number of faults incurred, with the exception of the Shorthand Speed Skills and Speed Keying units, which will state the words per minute speed achieved on the certificate.

Units

Details of the unit contents for Text Processing, Word Processing and Audio-Transcription at Level 1 are provided in this book.

The flexibility of qualifications within the Qualifications & Credit Framework means that candidates may take units at a higher or lower level than the level of their full qualification. The percentages allowed are described in the rules of combination contained within the table for each qualification.

Group 1: core units

06966	Text Production	4 credits
03945	Cynhyrchu Testun	4 credits
00004	Text Production (Screen Reader)	4 credits

Group 2: optional units

Level 1 Text Processing units

06967	Audio-Transcription	4 credits
06969	Computer Keyboard Skills	3 credits
06972	Shorthand Speed Skills	4 credits
06973	Speed Keying	4 credits
06971	Mailmerge	4 credits
06970	Legal Text Processing	4 credits
06968	Business Presentations	4 credits
06974	Word Processing	4 credits
03946	Prosesu Geiriau	4 credits

Level 1 iTQ units (Scheme 06611, Test and Trial units only)

T/500/7286	Email	2 credits
K/500/7303	Presentation Software	4 credits
J/500/7292	Word Processing Software	4 credits

At the time of printing, the new QCF iTQ units cannot be used for Text Processing (Business Professional) qualifications

Level 2 Text Processing units

06976	Audio-Transcription	4 credits
06977	Business Presentations	5 credits
06978	Document Presentation	5 credits
06980	Legal Audio-Transcription	5 credits
06994	Mailmerge	5 credits
06995	Medical Audio-Transcription	5 credits
06996	Medical Word Processing	5 credits
06997	Shorthand Speed Skills	5 credits
06998	Speed Keying	4 credits
06999	Word Processing	5 credits
03948	Prosesu Geiriau	5 credits

Level 2 iTQ units (Scheme 06611, Test and Trial units only)

F/500/7288	Email	4 credits
M/500/7304	Presentation Software	6 credits
H/500/6781	Word Processing Software	6 credits

At the time of printing, the new QCF iTQ units cannot be used for Text Processing (Business Professional) qualifications

Group 3: optional units

Entry Level Text Processing unit

06965	Speed Keying	2 credits

Unit contents

The following syllabuses give details of the unit contents for Text Production, Word Processing and Audio-Transcription at Level 1. They are updated from time to time by OCR and the current versions are available on the OCR website at www.ocr.org.uk.

The first section of each syllabus covers the following aspects.

- **Learning outcomes:** listed in the first column of the table, these describe the tasks that you will be able to carry out once you have acquired the necessary skills to complete the exam at this level.
- **Assessment criteria:** described in the second column of the table, they show the way in which your skills will be assessed in the exam.
- **Knowledge, understanding and skills:** detailed in the third column of the table, they describe the information you need to enable you to complete the exam.

The second section of each document covers the following:

- Unit aim
- Assessment
- Administration guidance
- Guidance on assessment and evidence requirements.

The third section of each document covers the following:

- **Marking criteria:** described in the first column of the table, they show the ways in which your work will be assessed.
- **Tutor notes:** listed in the second column of the table, these give further details about how an exam is marked. Although drafted for tutors, this information will give you invaluable help when you are working towards the exam.

OCR

RECOGNISING ACHIEVEMENT

TEXT PROCESSING (BUSINESS PROFESSIONAL)

Text Production

06966

Level:	1
Credits:	4
Learning Time:	40 hours

Learning Outcomes	Assessment Criteria	Knowledge, understanding and skills
1 Use a word processor or a typewriter efficiently	1.1 Use the different functions of a word processor or different parts of a typewriter	• Set top and left margins of at least 13 mm • Alter linespacing (single/double) as instructed • Emphasise text as instructed
2 Enter and format text from handwritten and typewritten drafts	2.1 Produce text accurately and efficiently from manuscript and typescript drafts	• Plan and organise work within deadlines • Read and transcribe variable quality manuscript • Plan layout of work in a variety of formats • Accurately key in text from handwritten and typewritten drafts • Interpret written instructions • Check accuracy of amendments and that all instructions have been carried out correctly • Proofread and correct errors, using appropriate correction techniques, to ensure work is 100% accurate • Use consistent style and format of presentation with at least one clear linespace before and after separate items within a document • Use appropriate stationery • Use English and mother-tongue dictionaries

3 Produce three business documents	3.1 Key in and print a business letter on pre-printed letterhead or by use of a template from handwritten draft	• Use conventional layout and style of a business letter • Insert today's date on letter • Use OCR supplied letterhead template • Key in *Our ref* details as shown in draft, including capitalisation • Indicate enclosure(s) as necessary according to the draft
	3.2 Key in and print a menu/notice/advert from handwritten draft	• Use conventional and consistent layout and style of a variety of business documents • Emphasise text, as instructed
	3.3 Key in and print an article or report from handwritten and typewritten draft	• Use conventional layout and style of a report or article • Use single/double linespacing as instructed
	3.4 Amend text as instructed	Amend text as shown in draft: • deletion with replacement words • deletion without replacement words • Follow correction signs:

new paragraph ⌐ or //

run on

insertion ⋏ with word(s) above or balloon with arrow eg

transpose horizontally ∽ or balloon with arrow eg

transpose vertically

stet – – – – – – with ✓ in margin

} no marginal instructions

	3.5 Expand abbreviations, ensuring correct spellings	Expand abbreviations shown in the list below:

a/c(s)	account(s)	org(s)	organisation(s)
approx	approximate(ly)	poss	possible
cat(s)	catalogue(s)	ref(s)	reference(s)
co(s)	company(ies)	ref(d)	refer(red)
dr	dear	sec(s)	secretary(ies)
doc(s)	document(s)	sig(s)	signature(s)
info	information	tel	telephone
mtg(s)	meeting(s)	temp	temporary
misc	miscellaneous	yr(s)	year(s)
necy	necessary	yr(s)	your(s)
opp(s)	opportunity(ies)		

days of the week (eg Thur, Fri)
months of the year (eg Jan, Feb)
words in addresses (eg Rd, St, Ave, Dr, Sq, Cres, Pl, Pk)
complimentary close (eg ffly, sncly)

	3.6 Check and correct material containing typographical errors, errors of agreement, punctuation and spelling errors	Correct errors in words that have been circled: • typographical errors including words containing extra, omitted and transposed letters and extraneous symbols • errors of agreement including those of subject/verb and quantity/noun • punctuation errors including omitted full stop and omitted initial capital at the start of a sentence • apostrophe errors including misplaced and superfluous apostrophes • spelling errors in words given below including their derivations where marked * eg plurals, prefixes (such as un-, in-, dis-, ir-) and suffixes (such as -ed, -ing, -ment, -tion, -ly, -able, -ible, -ence, -ial):

accommodate*	experience*
acknowledge*	finance*
advertise*	foreign
appreciate*	govern*
believe*	convenient*
business*	receipt*
client*	receive*
colleague*	recommend*
correspond*	separate*
definite*	sufficient*
develop*	temporary*
expense*	through

	3.7 Locate information from a resource sheet to include in a document	• Key in a piece of information (such as a name or job title) that will be found in a resource sheet

Unit aim

This unit aims to equip candidates with the ability to produce, from handwritten and typewritten draft material, a variety of routine business documents to a standard that meets the business document production requirements of employment.

Assessment

Assessment will consist of producing three business documents totalling 540 words and will take the form of a 1 hour 15 minute test set and marked by OCR.

Results will be graded Distinction, Pass or Fail.

To achieve a Distinction, candidates must produce the documents with no more than 3 faults within the time allowed (1 hour 15 minutes).

To achieve a Pass, candidates must produce the documents with no more than 8 faults within the time allowed (1 hour 15 minutes).

The grade achieved will be stated on the certificate.

Administration guidance

- Either a word processor or a typewriter may be used to complete the exam.

- Stationery: A4 plain paper. Pre-printed templates will be required for those candidates using a typewriter.

- Printing: candidates **must** carry out their own printing.

- For further information regarding administration for this qualification, please refer to the OCR document '*Administrative Guide for Vocational Qualifications*' (A850).

Guidance on assessment and evidence requirements

Candidates must produce three business documents to a standard acceptable in the workplace and outcomes must be within the permitted error tolerance.

Penalties are given for errors and the same fault appearing more than once will incur a penalty each time. One fault only will be given to any one word* irrespective of the number of errors that may appear in that word. For example, "miscellaneous" keyed in as "miss-selanious" will be penalised 1 fault, even though several faults have been incurred in the word.

* A word is defined as any normally recognisable word including a hyphenated word and associated punctuation and spacing. Other items that are treated as a word are:

- postcode
- initials and courtesy titles
- simple or complex numbers including money and times
- simple or compound measurements

You should refer to the '*OCR Administrative Guide to Vocational Qualifications (A850)*' for *Notes on Preventing Computer-Assisted Malpractice.*

Errors will be divided into 4 categories:

Marking Criteria	Tutor Notes
Section 1 Faults - keying in errors **One fault will be given for each word* which:**	
1.1 contains a character which is incorrect (including upper case character within a word), or is illegible for any reason	• A penalty will be incurred for any word that contains a character that is incorrect or that includes an upper case character within a word, eg *LaBel* • Candidates may use English and mother tongue dictionaries and spellcheckers where available
1.2 has omitted or additional characters or spaces (including omissions caused by faulty use of correction materials/ techniques, eg hole in paper)	• A space inserted between a word and its associated punctuation, eg *word :* or *word ?* will incur 1 fault per instance • Incorrect or omitted paired punctuation, eg brackets, single quotes will incur 1 fault per 'pair', eg (Progress Group), ' Progress Group '
1.3 contains handwritten character(s)	
1.4 has no space following it	
1.5 has more than 2 character spaces following it, except where appropriate, eg before postcode, after punctuation	In continuous text, 1 fault per instance will be incurred for: • more than 3 spaces appearing after a full stop, question mark, exclamation mark or colon • more than 2 spaces appearing after a comma, semi-colon, closing bracket, dash, apostrophe (at the end of a word) and closing single or double quotes • where a short line appears, this will be penalised if the first word following could have fitted at the end of the short line with at least 18 mm (¾") to spare (measuring the short line against the longest line in the document)
1.6 contains overtyping, including overtyping of pre-printed material (per entry regardless of the number of words involved) eg text cutting through letterhead template	

1.7 does not contain initial capitals:
  - as presented in the draft
  - for the first letter of a sentence
	• Candidates should key in text as presented in the draft. One fault per instance will be incurred for each initial capital drafted that has been keyed in as a lower case character
	• Failure to insert a capital letter following a penalty for an omitted full stop will not be penalised.
	• Inserting a capital letter following a penalty for an incorrect full stop will not be penalised

Section 2 Faults - omissions and additions **One fault will be given for:**	
2.1 each word which is the wrong word and a word that has been omitted or added or not removed as instructed (eg a word which is crossed out in the draft)	• *Our ref* details must be keyed as shown in the draft, including capitalisation. Treat the whole reference as one unit for marking purposes. Errors in references incur one fault maximum per document. Candidates will incur one fault if they set up their own reference, or omit the reference or add their own initials to the reference • In the letter the reference, date, name and address may be presented in any order but must appear above the salutation and must be keyed in as draft, including capitalisation • Any style of date is acceptable, with the exception of the American numeric format, eg *12/25/2009* as Christmas Day • Dates should appear below the letterhead and above the salutation of the letter and should have a clear linespace above/below • Dates will not be acceptable in the header/footer details alone • One fault will be incurred for each instance of a missing, incomplete or incorrect date to be inserted on correspondence as instructed on the front cover of the question paper • All errors in other dates are penalised per element • If a date appears in a document that does not require dating, this will be penalised 1 fault maximum unless the date appears as part of the personal details or above the first line of the document or below the last line of the document **Abbreviations** Abbreviations in handwritten draft should be expanded correctly; failure to do so is penalised 1 fault per word (as shown in 3.6 on page 3)
2.2 not applicable to this unit	

2.3 omission of implied or explicit instructions (regardless of the number of words involved) for failure to: - indicate an enclosure - underline text	• Where enclosures are implied, any appropriate method of indicating them may be used, eg *Enc Att Encs Atts*. Indications must differentiate between single and multiple enclosures • The indication of an enclosure must appear between the signatory details and the footer • Failure to underline a word or words within the text as shown in the draft incurs 1 fault • If underlining is too short or too long, a penalty under 1.2 will be incurred. (This is not treated as presentation which relates to the underlining of <u>headings</u> – see 4J below)

Section 3 Faults - transpositions and misplacements
One fault will be given for each instance of:

3.1 items not transposed (horizontally or vertically) in accordance with a correction sign	• Failure to transpose items horizontally or vertically will be penalised 1 fault maximum per correction sign
3.2 words that are misplaced within text, where there is no instruction	• Words inserted in the wrong order or place in the absence of an instruction eg misplaced within text or as foot or marginal note, regardless of the amount of material involved (in addition to any faults that may be incurred above)
3.3 failure to paragraph as per draft or as specified by a correction sign, eg new paragraph or run on	

Section 4 Faults – presentation
No more than one fault per paper for each of the following items:

4A left and/or top margins of less than 13 mm, or ragged left margin	This includes: • ragged left margin, eg additional character spacing at the beginning of a line or paragraph • main and subheadings not keyed in at the left margin, as presented in draft – unless otherwise instructed (eg centring)
4B no clear linespace before and after separate items within a document	• Failure to leave a clear linespace before and after separate items within a document, eg before/after headings, between paragraphs NB: Where letterhead template is centred or right aligned there is no requirement for a clear linespace below the letterhead. Where letterhead is left aligned a clear linespace must be left
4C failure to use linespacing as instructed	This includes: • failure to change linespacing as instructed

4D failure to emphasise text as instructed	This includes: <ul><li>emphasis extended beyond the required portion</li><li>additional emphasis of text where not requested (except for headings – see 4J below)</li></ul> Emphasis may be any method such as bold, italics, underlining, capitals, centring, change of font/size
4E not applicable to this unit	
4F not applicable to this unit	
4G work which is creased, torn or dirty (including conspicuous corrections)	<ul><li>Invigilators should report any machine problems resulting in marks on paper</li><li>Invigilators should also report any problems with printers, so as not to disadvantage candidates</li></ul>
4H incorrect stationery used (ie supplied letterhead, A4 plain paper)	<ul><li>Failure to use OCR supplied templates</li><li>Templates must not be altered in any way</li></ul>
4I inconsistent spacing between and within similar items within a document	<ul><li>Inconsistent spacing (including linespacing) between and within similar items is only penalised if a comparison with a similar item can be made within the same document</li><li>Inconsistent linespacing above and below an item, for example, an inset portion, will not be penalised as there is no further instance of insetting within the same document for comparison</li></ul>
4J use of initial capitals where not presented in draft, or: <ul><li>closed capitals used where not presented in draft, or</li><li>failure to use closed capitals as presented in draft, or</li><li>failure to key in headings with initial capitals and underlined as presented in draft</li></ul>	This includes: <ul><li>use of initial capitals where initial capitals were not presented in draft, eg *Sincerely* in complimentary close</li><li>closed capitals used where not presented in draft, eg *WHITE* instead of *White*</li><li>failure to use closed capitals as presented in draft, eg *DISEASES* keyed in as *Diseases*</li><li>failure to underline headings, including subheadings, as presented in the draft, eg "<u>Miscellaneous Household Items</u>" keyed in as "Miscellaneous Household Items"</li><li>capitalisation faults in postcodes</li></ul> Candidates should key in data exactly as shown in the draft (except for circled words with typographical errors, errors of agreement, punctuation and spelling errors) but additional emboldening, italicising or underlining of headings will not be penalised

4K inconsistent use of alternative spellings within a document	• Alternative spellings that may be found in an English dictionary will be accepted but a penalty will be incurred if that alternative spelling is used inconsistently, eg *organize* but *organisation* within the same document

4L inconsistent display of dates, measurements, weights, times, money, figures, dashes/hyphens	• Dates must be of consistent style throughout a document. For example, if full style is used such as *12 January 2009*, this style should be used for all subsequent dates within the same document. (Please also refer to Section 2.1 Notes above)
	
	• Measurements and weights must be used consistently. For example, *5cm* or *5 cm*; *16kg* or *16 kg*
	
	• Times should be keyed in as shown in the draft. Candidates should not change times from 12-hour clock to 24-hour clock or vice versa, unless instructed to do so
	
	• Money: there must be no character space between £ and the amount, eg *£60*
	
	• The display of figures should be an "acceptable system", eg
	  – all figures including "1"
	  – all words (but use of words such as *twenty-five* or *twenty five* must be consistent)
	  – *one* as a word, all others as figures
	  – *one* to *nine* or *ten* as words and then *10* or *11* upwards as figures
	  – *one* to *twenty* as words and then *21* upwards as figures
	
	• Where dashes or hyphens are used to represent the word "to" (eg *15-22* or *15 – 22*) these must be used consistently throughout a document

4M inconsistent use of open or full punctuation within a document	This includes: • a full stop appearing in any abbreviation such as enc, cc, eg, am, when open punctuation has been used • a missing full stop in any abbreviation such as enc., c.c., e.g. a.m., when full punctuation has been used
4N insertion of an additional comma which alters the meaning of a sentence	• Candidates should key in punctuation as presented in the draft. However, the insertion of an additional comma will only be penalised if this alters the meaning of the sentence

TEXT PROCESSING
(BUSINESS PROFESSIONAL)

Word Processing
06974

RECOGNISING ACHIEVEMENT

Level:	1
Credits:	4
Learning Time:	40 hours

Learning Outcomes	Assessment Criteria	Knowledge, understanding and skills
1 Use a word processor efficiently	1.1 Use the different functions of a word processor	• Ensure left and top margins of at least 13 mm • Underline text • Insert borders • Use spellchecker • Print documents on A4 plain paper
2 Input text from handwritten and typewritten drafts	2.1 Produce text accurately and efficiently from handwritten and typewritten drafts and print documents	• Plan and organise work within deadlines • Read and transcribe variable quality manuscript • Plan layout of work in a variety of formats • Accurately key in text from handwritten and typewritten drafts • Use English and mother-tongue dictionaries • Interpret written instructions • Use consistent style and format of presentation with at least one clear linespace before and after separate items within a document • Use appropriate stationery, ie plain A4 paper • Check accuracy of amendments and that all instructions have been carried out correctly • Proofread and correct errors

Learning Outcomes	Assessment Criteria	Knowledge, understanding and skills

	2.2 Amend text as instructed	• Amend text as shown in draft:
		  _ deletion with replacement words
		  _ deletion without replacement words
		Follow correction signs
		
		New paragraph $\lceil$ or $/\!/$
		Run on
		Insertion with word(s) above
		or balloon with arrow eg
		Transpose horizontally
		or balloon with arrow eg
		Transpose vertically
		
		Stet – – – – – with ✓ in margin

3 Produce four business documents totalling no more than 680 words (325 words to be input and no more than 355 words to be recalled) in the time allowed (1 hour 30 minutes)	3.1 Retrieve a report/article/information sheet, amend and print as instructed	• Retrieve text from pre-stored file • Adjust left margin • Change text to full justification throughout the document • Move text • Change linespacing of one paragraph to double linespacing, as instructed • Inset a paragraph of text from the left margin • Use software facilities to perform a word count on the task • Key in word count below final line of text • Insert an automatic filename and path in the footer area
	3.2 Recall a poster/advertisement/notice, amend text and print as instructed	• Retrieve text from pre-stored file • Ensure left and top margins are at least 13 mm • Insert a picture eg clip art • Emphasise a section of text

Learning Outcomes	Assessment Criteria	Knowledge, understanding and skills
		• Insert a full-page border • Centre one or more lines of text • Underline words which will be included in handwritten text in the draft
	3.3 Retrieve a document containing data and key in a table from handwritten draft, amend and print as instructed	• Retrieve text from pre-stored file • Ensure left and top margins are at least 13 mm • Key in a table from handwritten draft, which will not include ruling but candidates may insert lines of ruling if desired • Key in three columns of data – two containing text and one of figures • Key in a main heading and column headings in all capitals • Ensure data in columns and column headings are left aligned consistently • Carry out an aspect of modification, eg change the sequence of columns
	3.4 Retrieve a form and complete details given and print as instructed	• Retrieve a pre-stored form • Ensure left and top margins are at least 13 mm • Complete the pre-stored form from information given in handwritten draft • Ensure data on the form is aligned to the left consistently • Use the strikethrough facility to denote a deletion • Insert today's date

Unit aim

This unit aims to equip candidates with the ability to produce, from handwritten draft and recalled text, using a word processor, four routine business documents to a standard that meets the requirements of employment.

Assessment

Assessment will consist of producing four business documents totalling no more than 680 words (325 words to be input by candidates and no more than 355 recalled words) and will take the form of a 1 hour 30 minute test set and marked by OCR.

Results will be graded Distinction, Pass or Fail.

To achieve a Distinction, candidates must produce the documents with no more than 3 faults within the time allowed (1 hour 30 minutes).

To achieve a Pass, candidates must produce the documents with no more than 7 faults within the time allowed (1 hour 30 minutes).

The grade achieved will be stated on the certificate.

Administration guidance

- Word processing equipment **must** be used to complete the exam.

- Centres must ensure that the recall material for this examination is available for candidates. This recall material will be available on CD-ROM provided by OCR or can be downloaded from Interchange, OCR's secure website.

- Centres **must not** re-key or amend the pre-stored documents.

- Stationery: A4 plain paper will be required.

- Printing: Candidates **must** carry out their own printing.

- For further information regarding administration for this qualification, please refer to the OCR document '*Administrative Guide for Vocational Qualifications*' (A850).

Guidance on assessment and evidence requirements

Candidates must produce four business documents to a standard acceptable in the workplace and outcomes must be within the permitted error tolerance.

Penalties are given for errors and the same fault appearing more than once will incur a penalty each time. One fault only will be given to any one word* irrespective of the number of errors that may appear in that word. For example, "miscellaneous" keyed in as "miss-selanious" will be penalised 1 fault, even though several faults have been incurred in the word.

* A word is defined as any normally recognisable word including a hyphenated word and associated punctuation and spacing. Other items that are treated as a word are:

- postcode
- initials and courtesy titles

- simple or complex numbers including money, times and telephone numbers
- simple or compound measurements

You should refer to the '*OCR Administrative Guide to Vocational Qualifications* (A850)' for *Notes on Preventing Computer-Assisted Malpractice.*

Errors will be divided into 4 categories:

Marking Criteria	Tutor Notes
Section 1 Faults - keying in errors	
One fault will be given for each word* which:	
1.1 contains a character which is incorrect (including upper case character within a word), or is illegible for any reason	• A penalty will be incurred for any word that contains a character that is incorrect or that includes an upper case character within a word, eg *LaBel* • Candidates may use English and mother-tongue dictionaries and spellcheckers where available
1.2 has omitted or additional characters or spaces (including omissions caused by faulty use of correction materials/techniques, eg hole in paper)	• A space inserted between a word and its associated punctuation, eg *word :* or *word ?* will incur 1 fault per instance • Incorrect or omitted paired punctuation eg brackets, single quotes will incur 1 fault per 'pair', eg (Progress Group), 'Progress Group'
1.3 contains handwritten character(s)	
1.4 has no space following it	
1.5 has more than 2 character spaces following it, except where appropriate, eg before postcode, after punctuation No need for consistency after punctuation	In continuous text, 1 fault per instance will be incurred for: • more than 3 spaces appearing after a full stop, question mark, exclamation mark or colon • more than 2 spaces appearing after a comma, semi-colon, closing bracket, dash, apostrophe (at the end of a word) and closing single or double quotes • where a short line appears, this will be penalised if the first word following could have fitted at the end of the short line with at least 18 mm (¾") to spare (measuring the short line against the longest line in the document) NB: No penalty will be incurred for inconsistency after punctuation eg 1 or 2 spaces inconsistently after a full stop
1.6 contains overtyping, including overtyping of pre-printed material (per entry regardless of the number of words involved) eg text cutting through lines on the form	
1.7 does not contain initial capitals as presented in the draft, including the first letter of a sentence and the first letter of a row of text in a table	• Candidates should key in text as presented in the draft. One fault per instance will be incurred for each initial capital drafted that has been keyed in as a lower case character

Marking Criteria	Tutor Notes
	• Failure to insert a capital letter following a penalty for an omitted full stop will not be penalised. Likewise inserting a capital letter following a penalty for an incorrect full stop will not be penalised
Section 2 Faults – omissions and additions **One fault will be given for:**	
2.1 each word which is the wrong word and a word that has been omitted or added or not removed as instructed (eg a word which is crossed out in the draft)	• Failure to delete recalled text and insert replacement words will incur 1 fault for each word that has been omitted or is the wrong word • The unspecified deletion and/or duplication of recalled text will incur 1 fault per word, unless it can be attributed to a vertical or horizontal transposition, deletion without replacement (see 2.2 below), or move • If items to be vertically transposed include an amendment to text (eg deletion with replacement words) or a correction sign for insertion of words (eg caret sign, balloon or "stet"), 1 fault per word for wrong/omitted words will be incurred under 2.1, in addition to any penalty under 3.1 • Today's date should be inserted on the form, in the appropriate space, unless otherwise instructed • One fault will be incurred for each instance of a missing, incomplete or incorrect date to be inserted on correspondence as instructed on the front cover of the question paper • All errors in other dates are penalised per element • Any style of date is acceptable, with the exception of the American numerical format, eg *12/25/2009* as Christmas Day If a date appears in a document that does not require dating, this will be penalised 1 fault maximum unless the date appears as part of the personal details or above the first line of the document or below the last line of the document
2.2 each instance of failure to delete recalled text as instructed	• Failure to delete recalled text as shown in the draft will incur 1 fault maximum, irrespective of the number of words involved This relates to a deletion where there are no replacement words written above the words crossed through
2.3 omission of implied or explicit instructions (regardless of the number of words involved) for failure to: – ensure consistent use of font style/size throughout a document	• Changes made to the font style/size in a document where there is no instruction to do so will incur 1 fault maximum per exam paper • Save documents using filenames as instructed • Both the automatic filename and path must be clearly shown in the footer area; otherwise 1 fault maximum will be incurred
Marking Criteria	**Tutor Notes**

– insert an automatic filename and path in the footer area	• Any font style and size may be used in the footer area
– insert a picture	• Any picture may be used including clipart, from any source but candidates should re-size if necessary to ensure that all the text will fit on to one side of a sheet of A4 paper
– insert a full-page border	
– use software facilities to perform a word count	
– insert the total word count	• The picture may be positioned anywhere across the page but must appear in the correct position vertically
– underline text	
– carry out an aspect of modification	• Inserting a border that is not full-page will incur 1 fault
– use the strikethrough facility to show deletion of a word	• Any style of full-page border may be used
	• The word count will be evidenced by candidates keying in the figure below the final line of text
	• An incorrect word count will incur 1 fault maximum, eg candidates perform the word count at the wrong time
	• An incorrect word count resulting from errors in the text will not be penalised
	• Failure to underline words within the text exactly as shown in the draft incurs 1 fault maximum, including omission of the underline and underlining which is too long or too short
	(This is not treated as presentation which relates to the underlining of <u>headings</u> – see 4J below)
	• Failure to carry out an aspect of modification, eg change the sequence of columns in a table, will incur 1 fault
	• The strikethrough facility must be used to show deletion of the specified word in the form and this may be a single or double strikethrough
	• The words '*Delete as appropriate using strikethrough' on the form should not be deleted, but the candidate will not be penalised if they delete these words
	• Omitted or additional ruling in the form will be penalised one fault maximum
	• No clear linespacing and/or inconsistent linespacing between text and horizontal lines of ruling in the form will be accepted

Section 3 Faults - transpositions and misplacements

One fault will be given for each instance of:

3.1 items not transposed (horizontally or vertically) in accordance with a correction sign	• Failure to transpose items in recalled text (horizontally or vertically) in accordance with an amendment sign will incur 1 fault per correction sign
	• Omitted or additional text resulting from an attempt at vertical or horizontal transposition of recalled text will be penalised 1 fault maximum

Marking Criteria	Tutor Notes
3.2 words that are misplaced within	• Data that is entered in the wrong position on the

	text, where there is no instruction	pre-stored form will incur 1 fault per instance
3.3	failure to paragraph as per draft or as specified by a correction sign, eg new paragraph or run on	

Section 4 Faults – presentation

No more than one fault per paper for each of the following items:

4A	left and/or top margins of less than 13 mm, or ragged left margin	• Ragged left margin, eg additional character spacing at the beginning of a line or paragraph • Main and subheadings not keyed in at the left margin, as presented in draft – unless otherwise instructed (eg centring) or recalled
4B	no clear linespace before and after separate items within a document	• Failure to leave a clear linespace before and after separate items within a document, eg before/after headings, between paragraphs • Where lines of ruling have been inserted in the table, a penalty under 4B will not be incurred for failure to leave a clear linespace below the column headings
4C	failure to use linespacing as instructed	• Failure to change linespacing as instructed
4D	failure to emphasise text as instructed	• Emphasis extended beyond the section of text specified • Additional emphasis of text in a document where not requested (except for headings – see 4J below) • Emphasis may be bold, italics, underlining, change of font style/size only • Failure to clearly change the font style or size of some text as instructed will incur a penalty. Note that if the changes are not clear, eg using similar sans serif fonts or changing the font size by one point, a penalty will be incurred
4E	not applicable to this unit	
4F	failure to centre text as instructed	• Failure to centre text as instructed to within 13 mm over the typing line
4G	work which is creased, torn or dirty (including conspicuous corrections)	• Invigilators should notify OCR of any machine faults resulting in marks on the paper • Invigilators should also report any problems with printers, so as not to disadvantage candidates
4H	incorrect stationery used (ie A4 plain paper portrait)	• Failure to use OCR supplied templates • Failure to produce continuation sheets on plain paper • Page 1 of a report may be produced on plain or headed paper • The format (eg width of columns, ruling) of the recalled form must not be altered in any way

Marking Criteria	Tutor Notes
4I inconsistent spacing between and within similar items within a document	• Inconsistent spacing (including linespacing) between and within similar items is only penalised if a comparison with a similar item can be made within the same document • Inconsistent linespacing above and below an item, for example an inset portion, will not be penalised as there is no further instance of insetting within the same document for comparison

4J use of initial capitals where not presented in draft, or
 	
   – closed capitals used where not presented in draft
   – failure to use closed capitals as presented in draft
   – failure to key in headings with initial capitals and underlined as presented in draft
	This includes:
	• Use of initial capitals where initial capitals were not presented in draft, eg *Sincerely* in complimentary close
	• closed capitals used where not presented in draft, eg *White* keyed in as *WHITE*
	• failure to use closed capitals as presented in draft, eg *DISEASES* keyed in as *Diseases*
	• failure to underline headings, including subheadings, as presented in the draft, eg "<u>Miscellaneous Household Items</u>" keyed in as "Miscellaneous Household Items"
	• Capitalisation faults in postcodes
	• Candidates should key in data exactly as shown in the draft but additional emboldening, italicising or underlining of headings will not be penalised

4K inconsistent use of alternative spellings within a document	• Alternative spellings that may be found in an English dictionary will be accepted but a penalty will be incurred if that alternative spelling is used inconsistently, eg *organize* but *organisation* within the same document
4L inconsistent display of dates, measurements, weights, times, money, figures, dashes/hyphens, lines of ruling within a document	• Dates must be of consistent style throughout a document. For example, if full style is used such as *12 January 2009*, this style should be used for all subsequent dates, including those that appear within recall text, within the same document. (Please also refer to Section 2.1 Notes above) • Measurements and weights must be used consistently. For example, *5 cm* or *5cm*, *16 kg* or *16kg* • Times must be keyed in consistently within a document eg *10.30am* and *2.30 pm* within the same document would incur a penalty. Candidates must ensure that times that they key in are consistent with those that appear in recalled text within a document. Candidates must not change times from 12-hour clock to 24-hour clock or vice versa unless instructed to do so

Marking Criteria	Tutor Notes
	• Money: there must be no character space between £ and the amount, eg £60. In columns and tables accept spacing between £ and amount
	• The display of figures should be an "acceptable system", eg
	– all figures including "1"
	– all words (but use of words such as *twenty-five* or *twenty five* must be consistent)
	– *one* as a word, all others as figures
	– *one* to *nine* or *ten* as words and then *10* or *11* upwards as figures
	– *one* to *twenty* as words and then *21* upwards as figures
	• Where dashes or hyphens are used to represent the word "to" (eg *15-22* or *15 – 22*) these must be used consistently throughout a document
	• Lines of ruling in a table – a candidate opting to use gridlines in a table will incur a penalty only if these result in empty cells. NB A row of empty cells below column headings in a table will be penalised
4M inconsistent use of open or full punctuation within a document	• Full stop appearing in any abbreviation such as Enc, CC, eg, am, when open punctuation has been used
	• Missing full stop in any abbreviation such as Enc., C.C., e.g., a.m., where full punctuation has been used
4N insertion of an additional comma which alters the meaning of a sentence	Candidates should key in punctuation as presented in the draft. However, the insertion of an additional comma will only be penalised if this alters the meaning of the sentence
4O not applicable to this unit	
4P – failure to align text and figures in columns to the left consistently – failure to align data vertically with column headings	This applies to both the table and the form
4S failure to justify text or data as instructed	A penalty will be incurred: • if the right margin is justified but the left margin is ragged • if justification used when a right ragged margin is requested
4T failure to adjust margins or line length as instructed	• Left margin must be adjusted as instructed, within a 3 mm tolerance • Adjusting other margins as well as or instead of the left margin will incur 1 fault

Marking Criteria	Tutor Notes
4U failure to inset from left margin as instructed	• The inset measurement must be exactly as instructed. If extra text has been incorrectly included within the insetting, a penalty will be incurred • Insetting the wrong section of text incurs 1 fault maximum

TEXT PROCESSING (BUSINESS PROFESSIONAL)

RECOGNISING ACHIEVEMENT

Audio-Transcription
06967

Level:	1
Credits:	4
Learning Time:	40 hours

Learning outcomes	Assessment criteria	Knowledge, understanding and skills
1 Use audio equipment, word processor or a typewriter effectively	1.1 Use the different functions of a word processor or different parts of the typewriter in coordination with audio equipment	• Set top and left margins of at least 13 mm • Alter linespacing (single/double) as instructed • Emphasise text as instructed eg emboldening, underlining, capitals, etc • Interpreting dictated text, eg knowledge of English grammar and correct spelling, use a spellchecker, etc • Understanding of verbal instructions for punctuation eg full stop (.) comma (,) oblique (/) etc
2 Enter and format text from recorded material	2.1 Produce text accurately and efficiently from Information Sheet and recorded material	• Plan and organise work within deadlines • Plan layout of work in a variety of formats • Accurately key in text from recorded speech • Interpret audio instructions • Proofread and correct errors, using appropriate correction techniques, to ensure work is 100% accurate • Use consistent style and format of presentation with at least one clear linespace before and after separate items within a document

			• Use appropriate stationery • Use English and mother-tongue dictionaries • Check accuracy of amendments and that all instructions have been carried out correctly
3	Produce business documents	3.1	Key in and print a business letter on a pre-printed letterhead or by use of a template from recorded material	• Use conventional and consistent layout and style of a business letter • Use OCR supplied letterhead template • *Our ref* detail is keyed in as shown on the information sheet, including capitalisation • Insert today's date on letter • Insert a subject heading as dictated • Indicate enclosure, as implied in the verbal instruction, using an acceptable convention
		3.2	Key in and print a memo or notice from recorded material	• Use conventional and consistent layout and style of a variety of business documents • Insert reference detail as given on the information sheet where appropriate (ie the memo) • Insert today's date against date heading on memo • Memo must be produced on OCR supplied template • Insert headings as dictated
		3.3	Key in and print a short article or report from recorded material	• Use conventional and consistent layout and style of a report or article • Use single/double linespacing as instructed • Insert a subject heading as dictated • Change linespacing as instructed • Emphasise text, as instructed eg emboldening, underlining, capitals

Unit aim

This unit aims to equip candidates with the ability to produce a variety of routine business documents to a standard that meets the business document production requirements of employment from recorded speech and information provided on the information sheet.

Assessment

Assessment will consist of producing three business documents totalling 480 words and will take the form of a 1 hour 15 minute test set and marked by OCR.

Candidates will be required to work from recorded speech to produce 3 documents. The dictation will be given by means of a recording played on equipment over which the candidates have individual control.

Results will be graded Distinction, Pass or Fail.

To achieve a Distinction, candidates must produce the documents with no more than 3 faults within the time allowed (1 hour 15 minutes).

To achieve a Pass, candidates must produce the documents with no more than 8 faults within the time allowed (1 hour 15 minutes).

The grade achieved will be stated on the certificate.

Administration guidance

• Either a word processor or a typewriter may be used to complete the exam.

• Dictation for Audio-Transcription is recorded and supplied by OCR as mp3 and .wav files on CD-ROM and downloadable from OCR Interchange. The material must be copied onto equipment over which the candidates have individual control.

• Stationery: A4 plain paper. Pre-printed letterheads will be required for those candidates not using a typewriter.

• Printing: Candidates must carry out their own printing.

• Audio equipment to be supplied by the Centre.

• For further information regarding administration for this qualification, please refer to the OCR document 'Administrative Guide for Vocational Qualifications' (A850).

Guidance on assessment and evidence requirements

Candidates must produce three business documents to a standard acceptable in the workplace and outcomes must be within the permitted error tolerance.

Penalties are given for errors and the same fault appearing more than once will incur a penalty each time. One fault only will be given to any one word* irrespective of the number of errors that may appear in that word. For example "miscellaneous" keyed in as "miss-selanious" will be penalised 1 fault, even though several faults have been incurred in the word.

* A word is defined as any normally recognisable word including a hyphenated word and associated punctuation and spacing. Other items that are treated as a word are:

- postcode
- initials and courtesy titles
- simple or complex numbers including money, times and telephone numbers
- simple or compound measurements

You should refer to the 'OCR Administrative Guide to Vocational Qualifications (A850)' for Notes on Preventing Computer-Assisted Malpractice.

Errors will be divided into 4 categories:

Marking Criteria	Tutor Notes
Section 1 Faults – keying in errors	
One fault will be given for each word* which:	
1.1 contains a character which is incorrect (including upper case character within a word), or is illegible for any reason	• A penalty will be incurred for any word that contains a character that is incorrect or that includes an upper case character within a word, eg *LaBel* • Candidates may use English and mother-tongue dictionaries and spellcheckers where available
1.2 has omitted or additional characters or spaces (including omissions caused by faulty use of correction materials/techniques, eg hole in paper)	• A space inserted between a word and its associated punctuation, eg *word :* or *word ?* will incur 1 fault per instance • Incorrect or omitted paired punctuation, eg brackets, single quotes will incur 1 fault per 'pair', eg (Progress Group), ' Progress Group '
1.3 contains handwritten character(s)	
1.4 has no space following it	
1.5 has more than 2 character spaces following it, except where appropriate, eg before postcode, after punctuation	In continuous text, 1 fault per instance will be incurred for: • more than 3 spaces appearing after a full stop, question mark, exclamation mark or colon • more than 2 spaces appearing after a comma, semi-colon, closing bracket, dash, apostrophe (at the end of a word) and closing single or double quotes • where a short line appears, this will be penalised if the first word following could have fitted at the end of the short line with at least 18 mm (¾") to spare (measuring the short line against the longest line in the document)

1.6	contains overtyping, including overtyping of pre-printed material (per entry regardless of the number of words involved) eg text cutting through letterhead template	

1.7	does not contain initial capitals:
	   – as presented on the information sheet
	   – for the first letter of a sentence
		• Candidates should key in text as dictated. One fault per instance will be incurred for each initial capital presented on the information sheet that has been keyed in as a lower case character
		
		• Initial capitals will not be dictated for proper nouns, or at the beginning of sentences. One fault per instance will be incurred for each initial capital that has been keyed in as a lower case character for proper nouns, or at the beginning of a sentence.
		
		• Failure to insert a capital letter following a penalty for an omitted full stop will not be penalised. Likewise, inserting a capital letter following a penalty for an incorrect full stop will not be penalised

Section 2 Faults – omissions and additions

One fault will be given for:

2.1	each word which is the wrong word and a word that has been omitted or added	• Any style of *Our ref* is acceptable, but candidates will incur a fault if they set up their own reference (not as dictated or on the information sheet), or omit the reference, or add their own initials to the reference • The reference, date, name and address may be presented in any order but must appear above the salutation and must be keyed in as given on the information sheet, including capitalisation • The subject heading must appear somewhere between the letterhead details and the first paragraph of the letter and must be keyed in as dictated • Any style of date is acceptable, with the exception of the American numerical format, eg *12/25/2009* as *Christmas Day* • Dates should appear below the letterhead and above the salutation of the letter and should have a clear linespace above/below • Dates will not be acceptable in the header/footer details alone • One fault will be incurred for each instance of a missing, incomplete or incorrect date to be inserted on correspondence as instructed on the front cover of the question paper • All errors in other dates are penalised per element • Where postdating is required, one fault maximum will be incurred for any errors or omissions

		•	If a date appears in a document that does not require dating, this will be penalised 1 fault max unless the date appears as part of the personal details or above the first line of the document or below the last line of the document
2.2	failure to indicate punctuation as dictated		

2.3	omission of implied or explicit instructions (regardless of the number of words involved) for failure to:
	  − insert a subject heading
	  − indicate an enclosure
		•	Errors or omission in a subject heading will incur 1 fault max

		•	Where enclosures are implied, any appropriate method of indicating them may be used, eg *Enc Att Encs Atts*. Indications must differentiate between single and multiple enclosures
		•	The indication of an enclosure must appear between the signatory details and the footer

Section 3 Faults – transpositions and misplacements

One fault will be given for each instance of:

3.1	not applicable to this unit		
3.2	words that are misplaced within text, where there is no instruction	This includes:	
		•	words inserted in the wrong order or place in the absence of an instruction eg misplaced within text or as foot or marginal note, regardless of the amount of material involved (in addition to any faults that may be incurred above)
		•	each incorrect insertion of an entry against a pre-printed or template item
3.3	failure to paragraph as per verbal instruction		

Section 4 Faults – presentation

No more than one fault per paper for each of the following items:

4A	left and/or top margins of less than 13 mm, or ragged left margin	This includes:	
		•	ragged left margin, eg additional character spacing at the beginning or a line or paragraph
		•	main heading not keyed in at the left margin, in the absence of an alternative instruction
4B	no clear linespace before and after separate items within a document	This includes:	
		•	failure to leave a clear linespace before and after separate items within a document, eg before/after headings, between paragraphs
		NB: Where the recall letterhead template is centred or right aligned there is no requirement for a clear linespace below the letterhead. Where letterhead template is left aligned a clear linespace **must** be left	
4C	failure to use linespacing as instructed	This includes:	
		•	failure to change linespacing as instructed

4D	failure to emphasise text as instructed	This includes: • emphasis extended beyond the required portion • additional emphasis of text where not requested (except for headings – see 4J below) Emphasis may be any method such as bold, italics or underlining
4E	not applicable to this unit	
4F	not applicable to this unit	
4G	work which is creased, torn or dirty (including conspicuous corrections)	• Invigilators should report any machine problems resulting in marks on paper • Invigilators should also report any problems with printers, so as not to disadvantage candidates
4H	incorrect stationery used (eg letterhead, A4 plain paper)	• The first page of a report may be produced on plain or headed paper • Failure to use OCR templates • Templates must not be altered in any way
4I	inconsistent spacing between and within similar items within a document	• Inconsistent spacing (including linespacing) between and within similar items is only penalised if a comparison with a similar item can be made within the same document • Inconsistent linespacing above and below an item, for example, an inset portion, will not be penalised as there is no further instance of insetting within the same document for comparison
4J	use of initial capitals where not presented on the information sheet or: • closed capitals used where not dictated • failure to use closed capitals as dictated • failure to key in headings with initial capitals • failure to underline as dictated	This includes: • use of initial capitals where initial capitals were not dictated eg *Sincerely* in complimentary close • headings with initial capitals acceptable as: Facilities in all Conference Rooms, or Facilities In All Conference Rooms • closed capitals where not dictated or presented on the information sheet eg *White* keyed in as *WHITE* • failure to use closed capitals as dictated eg *DISEASES* keyed in as *Diseases* • failure to underline headings, including subheadings, as dictated, eg "<u>Miscellaneous Household Items</u>" keyed in as "Miscellaneous Household Items" • capitalisation faults in postcodes Candidates should key in data exactly as dictated and as given on the information sheet but additional emboldening, italicising or underlining of headings will not be penalised

4K	inconsistent use of alternative spellings within a document	• Alternative spellings that may be found in an English dictionary will be accepted but a penalty will be incurred if that alternative spelling is used inconsistently, eg *organize* but *organisation* within the same document

4L	inconsistent display of dates, measurements, weights, times, money, figures, dashes/hyphens, lines of ruling within a document	• Dates must be of consistent style throughout a document. For example, if full style is used such as *12 January 2009*, this style should be used for all subsequent dates within the same document. (Please also refer to Section (2.1) Notes above)
		
		• Measurements and weights must be used consistently. For example, *5 cm* or *5cm*; *16 kg* or *16kg*
		
		• Times should be keyed in as dictated. Candidates should not change times from 12-hour clock to 24-hour clock or vice versa, unless instructed to do so
		
		• Money; there must be no character space between £ and the amount, eg *£60*. However, in columns and tables accept spacing between £ and amount
		
		• The display of figures should be an "acceptable system", eg
		  − all figures including "*1*"
		  − all words (but use of words such as *twenty-five* or *twenty five* must be consistent)
		  − *one* as a word, all others as figures
		  − *one* to *nine* or *ten* as words and the *10* or *11* upwards as figures
		  − *one* to *twenty* as words and then *21* upwards as figures
		
		• Where dashes or hyphens are used to represent the word "to" (eg 15-22 or 15 − 22) these must be used consistently throughout a document

4M	inconsistent use of open or full punctuation within a document	This includes: • a full stop appearing in any abbreviation such as enc cc eg am when open punctuation has been used • a missing full stop in any abbreviation such as enc. c.c. e.g. a.m. where full punctuation has been used
4N	insertion of an additional comma which alters the meaning of a sentence	• Candidates should key in punctuation as dictated. However, the insertion of an additional comma will only be penalised if this alters the meaning of the sentence

3 KNOWLEDGE, UNDERSTANDING AND SKILLS

This section provides explanatory notes and exercises for each of the types of document that appear in the OCR exams. The notes and exercises for each different exam unit are grouped together.

The exercises are similar to the tasks you will have to complete in the exams, with circled instructions at the top of each document similar to those in the exam papers.

Notes pages

Notes pages precede each set of exercises. They explain how you should lay out documents and how to deal with the editing instructions. Take the time to read and understand the notes relating to each set of exercises before attempting them. You can refer to the notes as you work through each exercise.

Practice exercises

There are three new practice exercises for each type of document. Recall text for these exercises is available on the Hodder Plus website (see below). Once you have completed an exercise, proofread it and correct any errors. Save it using the filename indicated and print a copy. Find the correct worked example of the exercise in the Worked Examples section and proofread your copy against this. If you are a member of a group, you may find it helpful to proofread each other's work.

Recall text from the Hodder Plus website

You will need to access files on the Hodder Plus website at **www.hodderplus.co.uk/ocrtextprocessing** in order to carry out the following:

- open and use letterhead and memo templates
- recall text and amend as instructed
- access dictation for the audio-transcription exercises and practice exams.

To access these files you will need to enter the following username and password:

username: text processing
password: recall1

The templates that you will need to recall for Text Production and Audio-Transcription are saved under the following filenames:

LETTERHEAD   MEMO

For the purpose of these exercises and practice exams, you may use the same letterhead for any of the Text Production or Audio-Transcription documents, although some of the worked examples may show different letterheads. The same applies to the other templates, where slight variations may occur.

The text that you will need to recall for Word Processing is saved under the filenames given to you in each document in the practice exercises and exams.

Audio-Transcription

The Candidate Information Sheets (containing proper nouns) are provided in this section. Dictated material is saved under filenames given to each exercise and accessed from the Hodder Plus website at **www.hodderplus.co.uk/ocrtextprocessing**.

TEXT PRODUCTION LEVEL 1 PRACTICE EXERCISES

WITH DETAILED NOTES ON HOW TO WORK THE FOLLOWING DOCUMENTS:

- Letter
- Menu
- Notice
- Advertisement
- Report
- Article

LETTERS

Layout and style of a business letter

You will be required to produce a business letter in the Text Production and Audio-Transcription exams. For these exercises, a letterhead template will be provided on the Hodder Plus website. The font style, size and position of this must be retained. The body of the text may be in a different font, but must be easy to read. Arial 11 or Times New Roman 12 are popular.

Open punctuation is used in OCR exams and in these exercises. This means that punctuation is inserted only where essential (eg full stops, apostrophes) or to clarify meaning (eg commas, brackets, dashes). Copy punctuation given in the draft, but look out for missing full stops or misplaced/superfluous apostrophes in the Text Production letter.

The sample letter that follows is in blocked style (each line starting at the left margin), apart from the letterhead, and is in open punctuation. This is the style used in OCR exams. There should be at least one clear linespace between each separate item, with equal spacing between paragraphs.

Date

You must date each letter with the date on which you take the exam. No instruction will be given in the draft, but a reminder is given on the front cover of the question paper. A good position for the date is before or after the reference, although other positions are acceptable. The following styles are all acceptable:

10 August 2009   10th August 09   August 10 2009   10 Aug 09   10.8.09
                        10/08/09   10/08/2009

The example that is all in figures is more suitable for forms. In this style of date, if the month is shown before the day (ie 8.10.09), a penalty will be incurred, as it could be read as 8 October 2009.

Reference

Our ref must be displayed as shown in the draft. Follow the spacing, punctuation and capitalisation when keying in the actual reference. Do not add your initials to a reference, or add a *Your ref*, as this will incur a penalty.

Special mark

You are not required to insert a special mark at Level 1.

Name and address

Follow the draft with regard to capitalisation. If the recipient's first name is drafted in full, that is how it should be keyed. Substituting an initial would be penalised.

Usual business practice is to show the name of the town in closed capitals, with the name of the county in initial capitals. In OCR exams and these exercises, abbreviations for *Drive, Street, Crescent*, and so on, should be expanded, but the county may remain abbreviated. (See 3.5 of the Text Production Syllabus in the Assessment Criteria section for a list of abbreviations to be expanded.) The postcode should be keyed with one space between its two parts. It may appear on a separate line or on the same line as the town/county and separated from it by several spaces, as follows:

Mr Sane Khor
Computer Courses
MANCHESTER   M5 2JT

Salutation and complimentary close

The salutation and complimentary close need to follow business practice. Do not mix the styles – *Dear Sir* should not be followed by *Yours sincerely*, but always by *Yours faithfully.* The styles should match, as shown below:

Dear Sir(s)/Madam …Yours faithfully
Dear Sane/Mr Khor …Yours sincerely

Leave at least four clear linespaces for the signature. If the letter runs into a second page, then at least two lines of text should be carried over to the continuation sheet, along with the complimentary close.

Enclosure(s)

If the text indicates that an item/items are being enclosed, attached or included, you must show this at the end of the letter below the signatory details. Any appropriate methods are acceptable but you must show clearly whether there are single or multiple enclosures, eg:

Enc/Encs   enc/encs   ENC/ENCS   Att/Atts   ATT/ATTS

Copies and routing

You will not be required to take extra copies at Level 1.

Continuation sheet

Where the letter goes on to a second page, that page should be printed on plain paper. It should also be numbered, but no other heading details need appear other than your candidate name and centre number.

Letterhead of Writer	**Progress Group** **Westwood Way** **COVENTRY** CV4 8JQ **024 7647 0033**

Date letter prepared

20 August 2009

Writer's reference

Our ref   AC/jpd/L208

Receiver's reference

Your ref   SK/098

Special mark

URGENT

Name and address of person to whom the letter is written

Mr Sane Khor
Computer Courses
MANCHESTER
M5 2JT

Salutation

Dear Mr Khor

Subject heading

TEXTBOOK ORDER KME L208

Paragraphs of text

Thank you for your order for the sets of the revised edition of Keyboarding Made Easy, which will be available in bookshops next week.

I have arranged for the copies to be dispatched to you by DPL. I trust this will meet your deadline. In the meantime, I am enclosing an advance copy, for your personal use.

You mentioned in your email that you are starting a new business course. You may find our current catalogue of interest, a copy of which is also enclosed. There is an excellent range of packages covering subjects such as the internet, desktop publishing, databases and spreadsheets.

Thank you for your custom and do not hesitate to contact us if we can be of further assistance.

Complimentary close

Yours sincerely

Space for signature of sender

Name of sender
Job title

April Chaplin
Sales Executive

Enclosure(s) indicated

Encs

Person to receive copy

Copy Eddie Lanteri
          File

Amendments to text in letter document

Alterations to text

Refer to page 9 of the Text Production Syllabus in the 'Assessment Criteria' section for the list of amendment and correction signs. Some of these will appear in the following exercises.

Abbreviations and spellings

In the Text Production exercises and exams abbreviations, which will not be circled, must be identified and expanded. Spelling errors will be circled and must be corrected. The lists of abbreviations and spellings given on page 10 of the Text Production Syllabus in the 'Assessment Criteria' section contain the only words that will be tested in this way in this unit. Abbreviations that do not appear on the list, such as Ltd, plc, NB, etc should not be expanded.

Apostrophe and punctuation errors

The apostrophe error will be circled for you to correct. It will be either mis-placed or superfluous.

There will be an omitted full stop or an omitted initial capital at the beginning of a sentence for you to correct. These errors will be circled.

Locate and include information

A Resource Sheet is provided for this test, in which only the initial letter of one word will be drafted in the document. You will need to find that word in the Resource Sheet so that you can complete the word in your document. It will be very obvious – for example, your draft may show *Mrs K_____* and the Resource Sheet will mention a *Mrs Krupps*. You then complete the word *Mrs Krupps* in your document.

EXERCISE TP 1.1

Our ref CD/WF

Miss N Burnton
17 Wessex Park Rd
BRISTOL
BS3 4NR

Dear Miss Burnton

We are writing to all our shareholders to give details about a
proposed company merger. We have pleasure
in enclosing an information pack. This will
provide answers to many of your questions. In
order for this merger to proceed it is
necy to have the support of our shareholders.
A vote will take place at the next monthly
meeting. This meeting will be at our head
office in B___ city centre. We will write to
you as soon as poss to let you know the
date and time of the meeting.

You will be able to vote by post or you may
attend the meeting in person. Your chairman
reccommends that you vote in favour of the
merger.

We firmly believe that this merger is in the
best interest's of our company. The merger
will allow us to expand our business into
many other countries. As a direct result consequence ✓
of the merger your company will become
financially secure.

We urge you to take the time to read the
information pack. Please use your vote wisely.

Yours sncly

Carol Dunne
Company Secretary

Enc

RESOURCE SHEET

DOCUMENT 1

This meeting will be at our head office in Bath city centre.

EXERCISE TP 1.2

Our ref MM/BC

Mrs C Richmond
52 Brandon Cres
TAVERHAM
Norfolk
NR8 2LK

Dr Carolyn

For some time now I have thought that a monthly newsletter would be a good way of passing on info to our volunteers. Enclosed is a copy of the first issue. I hope you will find it helpful. As you will see, details are included of the many training courses open to volunteers. The next course on fire safety will take place on the first T——— of next month. This course is mandatory. If you cannot attend on that day, there will be other dates later in the year when you can enrol for this worthwhile training.

I should be grateful if you would complete the tear-off slip at the foot of the newsletter. This is to ensure that your up-to-date details are on file. A contact number in case of an emergency is also required. Please leave your signed form in my pigeon hole when you are next on duty.

I should like to take this opp to say how much we appreciate the time and effort given by our volunteers week in week out.

Yours sincerely

Michelle Martin
Volunteer Co-ordinator

Enc

RESOURCE SHEET FOR DOCUMENT 1

The next course on fire safety will take place on the first Thursday of next month.

EXERCISE TP 1.3

Our ref HM/246

Ms Jayne Fielding
46 Sycamore St
LEICESTER
LE9 4TP

Dr Ms Fielding

Thank you for your recent enquiry about our storage units. I note that you will soon be leaving college to spend some time travelling and need a safe place to leave your belongings. We have a new storage facility in P__ Place. This is very close to your current address. You can rent a small unit for as little as £6 per week. The cost includes insurance and VAT. The unit's may be rented for an indefinite period if you pay by direct debit. We would recomend this method of payment if you plan to be out of the country for a long time.

Our units are open 24 hours a day so you have total freedom of access. Your ~~unique~~ personal PIN code will allow you to enter the compound at all times of the day and night.

If you would like to visit, please tel me on 443861. A member of my team will give you a guided tour of the facility and will explain how we operate.

I look forward to hearing from you soon.

Yrs sincerely

Harry Middleton
Client Support

RESOURCE SHEET

We have a new storage facility in Park Place.

MENU/NOTICE/ADVERTISEMENT

Layout and style

This document could be a menu, notice or advertisement and should be printed on plain A4 paper. Follow the layout indicated in the draft. Be careful to follow capitalisation as shown, particularly within lists.

Amendments to text

Refer to page 9 of the Text Production Syllabus in the 'Assessment Criteria' section for the list of amendment and correction signs. Some of these will appear in these documents.

Spellings

Spelling errors will be circled and must be corrected. The list of spellings given on page 10 of the Text Production Syllabus in the 'Assessment Criteria' section contains the only words that will be tested in this way in this unit.

Emphasis

You will be instructed to emphasise a portion of text. This is usually carried out by emboldening, using closed capitals or changing the font style/size. Make sure that you emphasise only the section indicated.

EXERCISE TP 1.4

PROGRESS GROUP

(BREAKFAST CONFERENCE MENU)　　(a wide variety of)

(THE RUBY RESTAURANT)

The restaurant is (convenently) situated on the ground floor of the hotel.

THE BUFFET

Help yourself to items from the buffet.

Cereals with hot or cold milk
Toast and marmalade
Cold meats and cheeses
Fresh fruit salads with yoghurt

COOKED BREAKFASTS　　(Emphasise this sentence)

Order hot food from the waiter.

Traditional cooked breakfast incwding tomatoes, bacon and eggs.

DRINKS

Tea and coffee will be served at your table by the waiter.

A selection of fruit juice ~~including orange and grapefruit juice~~ is available from the buffet.

EXERCISE TP 1.5

THE WHITE HORSE INN

CHEF'S RECCOMENDATIONS

(emphasise this heading)

STARTERS

Celery and stilton soup with croutons
Avocado and prawn cocktail
Smoked haddock mousse garnished with salad

MAIN COURSES

Our main courses are served with a choice of roast, chipped or mashed potatoes and fresh seasonal vegetables.

Oven-baked turkey
Roast leg of lamb with garlic and rosemary
Hungarian style pork chops ~~cooked in an orange sauce~~
Baked stuffed courgettes (vegetarian)

(marinated in a spicy apricot sauce)

DESSERTS

Pears in ginger wine
Fresh strawberry gateau filled with cream
Dutch apple tart with custard
Cheese and biscuits

Coffee and chocolate mints

EXERCISE TP 1.6

PROGRESS CENTRAL

The new dining (experence) in ▾Birmingham! Come
and join us for lunch and enjoy fabulous food
at our splendid waterside location.

(the middle of)

Our lunch menu includes

Leek and potato soup
(Chicken with tarragon sauce)
(Grilled goat's cheese on roasted peppers)
Lemon sole with grapes
Chocolate truffle cake
Lime and passion fruit mousse
(Emphasise this sentence)
Prices start at £8.50 for two courses. The service
charge is included.

For a limited period only, we are offering ~~all our clients~~
free coffee and mints with all orders.

Telephone us on 298754 for further details.

EXERCISE TP 1.7

HEALTH AND SAFETY ⟨to train at least six⟩

The health and safety of all our staff is very important.

We need more first aiders. We only have one person on each floor who has been trained in first aid.

⟨Emphasise this sentence⟩

Please let your manager know if you would like to be trained for this important role.

First aiders ⟨recieve⟩ a small increase in salary.

⟨At the end of the course there is an examination.⟩

⟨The training course lasts five days.⟩

The company would like ~~to have at least~~ two qualified first aiders on each floor.

EXERCISE TP 1.8

REFUSE COLLECTION

NOTICE TO HOUSEHOLDERS LIVING BETWEEN THE
OUTER RING ROAD AND THE CITY BOUNDARY

Please note that there will be a change in your
black bin collection day. Collections will now
take place one day later. This new scheme will
start next month.

Please ensure your bins are placed outside before
7 am on the correct day.

A calendar will be sent to you shortly.

The council regrets any inconveinence that this
new arrangement may cause. Please contact them
by telephone or email if you have a query.

emphasise this sentence

showing the new days
and times

EXERCISE TP 1.9

SALE OF LOST PROPERTY

Progress Trains would like to (advetise) our forthcoming lost property sales.

These will be held on the first Saturday of each month between 9.30 am and 11.30 am. at the East Midlands depot

(Emphasise this sentence)
All proceeds will go to charity.

Items to be sold include

Umbrellas, hats and scarves
Mobile phones
Paperback books
Glasses, purses and other personal items

Please support us. Visit our website www. progresstrains.com for additional information on the sales.

All goods have been left on Progress Trains. They have remained unclaimed for ~~a period of~~ at least six months.

EXERCISE TP 1.10

PROGRESS GROUP ESTATE AGENTS

We are very pleased to be able to offer for sale by public auction the property known as Upper Farm. (Emphasise this sentence)

There will be three (seperate) lots for auction.

LOT 1

THE FARMHOUSE

The farmhouse ~~is a listed building and~~ includes five bedrooms and a cellar.

(THE OUTBUILDINGS)

(of pasture which are currently)

(LOT 2)

There are four large wooden barns and a brick building which houses the milking equipment.

LOT 3

THE LAND

There are one hundred acres used for grazing cattle.

For further details please contact Progress Group Estate Agents.

EXERCISE TP 1.11

SEAWARD HOMES

emphasise this sentence

A select (developement) of 2, 3 and 4 bedroom homes is nearing completion. The show house is now open and can be viewed by appointment.

All homes come complete with fully fitted kitchens and carpets. Buyers will have a wide choice of quality and colour. The master bedroom has en suite facilities.

Further details can be found on www.seaward2.co.uk.

The sea is only a short walk away and the attractive town of Wells with all its amenities ~~and tourist attractions~~ is a few minutes by car.

on the North Norfolk coast

EXERCISE TP 1.12

IS STORAGE A PROBLEM?

Progress Storage has been providing our satisfied (cleints) with additional storage for over ten years. We are known for our excellent service.

Have you run out of space at home? If so, consider renting a storage unit from our firm.

Our modern units offer (to your personal possessions)

Clean and dry storage
Access†day and night
Very competitive rental charges
Town centre locations
(Emphasise this sentence)
If you would like ~~us to provide you with~~ further details of our services, please telephone 443861. Our helpful staff will be pleased to give you a quote.

REPORT/ARTICLE

Layout and style

This document should be printed on plain A4 paper and has been designed to fit on to one page.

Linespacing

Linespacing before and after headings and between paragraphs must be consistent within a document. You will be instructed to change the linespacing of a section of the text.

Headings

Follow the draft regarding capitalisation of headings. Leave at least one clear linespace before and after headings consistently. A heading should not be on a different page to the start of its related paragraph.

Amendments to text

Refer to page 9 of the Text Production Syllabus in the 'Assessment Criteria' section for the list of amendment and correction signs. Some of these will appear in these exercises.

Abbreviations and spellings

Abbreviations must be identified and expanded. They will not be circled. Spelling errors, which are circled, must be corrected. The lists of abbreviations and spellings given on page 10 of the Text Production Syllabus in the 'Assessment Criteria' section contain the only words that will be tested in this way in this unit. Abbreviations that do not appear on the list, such as Ltd, plc, NB, etc should not be expanded.

Typographical errors

These are words containing extra, omitted or transposed letters and extraneous symbols. The words containing typing errors are circled at this level and must be corrected.

Grammatical errors

There will be one error of agreement test in this document. It will be circled and must be corrected. It will be very obvious at this level, eg *he are, three teacher*.

Underline text

You will be required to underline one or two words of text as shown on the draft. Make sure that the underlining does not extend either side of the selected words, although it may include any punctuation that is part of the word.

This underlining would be penalised.

This underlining would be <u>correct</u>.

This underlining would also be <u>correct.</u>

EXERCISE TP 1.13

(Use single linespacing except where indicated)

SEARCH FOR NEW OFFICES

I have looked at three (building) in the centre of town. In addition, I have inspected an office close to the old trading estate on the outskirts of town. All of the buildings I have seen have some good and bad points. I did not (veiw) an office that met all our needs. I am told by local estate (agens) that premises of the size we require do not come onto the market very often.

(this paragraph only in double linespacing)

However, I think that the building in the High Street meets most of our needs. We should proceed by asking all the department heads to a mtg. They should arrange a date for a site visit early next week. We can then discuss a plan for the (space available) for each department.

need to make some changes to
We will ~~have to erect internal walls to change~~ the layout of the space if we decide to proceed with the purchase of the High (Stre4et) building.

The ground floor is one large space and this needs to be divided into smaller rooms. There is <u>no reception</u> and we would need to make a waiting area.

are cracked and
Most of the (fitttings) in the bathrooms need to be replaced. The kitchen units are very old and some of the cupboard doors are broken.

The estate agent told me that there were two other firms interested in buying this building for office use. I (recomend) that we instruct our surveyor to proceed with the survey as soon as poss.

EXERCISE TP 1.14

PROGRESS LANDSCAPES

TIPS FOR THE AMATEUR

use double line spacing except where indicated

This is the first of a series of articles aimed at helping amateurs to undetake simple jobs around the house and garden.

PAVING

These paragraphs only in single line spacing

Most paving is laid on sharp sand or on a bed of mortar. Advice should be sought if the area to be paved is subject to heavy use. It is wise to start lay7ing the slabs against a house/wall. *or garage* Then work outwards towards an edge that is flexible. This will avoid having to cut too many stones.

Should cutting be necy, a disc cutter or chisel is recommended. The choice will depend on the depth of the stone. Our co sells and hires out tools for this purpose.

It is most important to use a spirit level to make sure the slabs is even. They should always slope away from the house and garage to prevent flooding.

DECKING

Careful preparation is neeeded when laying decking. The cleared site should be marked out using pegs and string lines. Joists and deck posts must be placed underneath the decking. Screws then are fixed to secure the platform. All instructions should be read thruogh very carefully before starting the work.

SAFETY

It is sensible to wear gloves when handling wood to aviod splinters. Put on a mask to prevent inhaling sawdust and treated timbers. If using power tools, goggles are essential. These will help to protect the eyes.

give tips on how to build a greenhouse.
Our next article will ~~be on the construction of a water feature.~~

EXERCISE TP 1.15

PROGRESS MONEY

A SAFE INVESTMENT

Use double linespacing except where indicated

For your peace of mind during these uncertain times, why not invest your money with us?

Progress Money has a fine reputation for ~~securing our customers' financial security~~ *taking care of its clients' money*. Do not risk your money *with other, less reputable orgs when we can help your savings grow.*

One of our most poppular products *at the moment* is our 3-year fixed rate bond. This is desined for long-term investments. It offer an interest rate which is fixed for 3 years. *The smallest amount you can invest in this a/c is £1,000. There is no maximum amount. We are offering an interest rate of 3.75 per cent per annum. At the end of the term, the interest rate will match the Bank of England base rate.*

This paragraph only in single linespacing

If you take out this product, you should note that you are not allowed to withdraw any money during the first year. After this time you may take out all or part of your investment by cheque. However, you will lose interest on the invested sum.

Interest is worked out on a daily basis and you will receive it once a year.

Income tax may be deducted. Some peo%ple may be able to reclaim any tax paid. Check with your tax office if you are unsure.

Progress Money has branches across the Untied Kingdom. For details of your nearest branch, or to request a list of our products, please call Customer Services on 08081 579832. *We look forward to hearing from you.*

WORD PROCESSING LEVEL 1 PRACTICE EXERCISES

WITH DETAILED NOTES ON HOW TO WORK THE FOLLOWING DOCUMENTS:

- Report
- Article
- Information Sheet
- Poster
- Advertisement
- Notice
- Table
- Form

REPORT/ARTICLE/INFORMATION SHEET

Margins

In these exercises and the Word Processing exam you will be instructed to adjust the left margin of the document. Open the recall text, then use **File** ➤ **Page Setup** to adjust the margin. Make sure that *Apply to Whole Document* is flagged**.**

Justify text

You will be instructed to use full justification. To do this you need to highlight all the text using **Control + A** then click the **Justify** icon.

Inserting filename and path

You will be instructed to insert a filename and path in the footer of this document. Use **View** ➤ **Header and Footer** ➤ select **Footer** ➤ click **Insert Auto Text** ➤ select **Filename and Path**. When the data appear click **Close**.

Amendments to text

Refer to page 18 for the Word Processing Syllabus in the 'Assessment Criteria' section showing the list of amendment and correction signs. Some of these will appear in these exercises.

Change linespacing

You will be instructed to change the linespacing of one paragraph of text. The linespacing before and after that section should be consistent.

Inset text

When insetting a portion of text, it is important that the measurement is exact.

To inset from the left margin, select the relevant text and use **Format** ➤ **Paragraph** using the arrows in the left margin box to increase the paragraph indent.

Move text

To **Move** a section of text, highlight it and use the **Cut** and **Paste** icons. That portion of text should appear only once in the document. To ensure consistency, it may be necessary to adjust the linespacing once you have completed a move.

Word count

Leave the word count until the very end, once you have proofread your document and saved the correct version. To perform an automatic word count, use **Tools** ➤ **Word Count** and the number of words will be displayed in the dialogue box. Make a note of this number, leave a clear linespace after the last line of text in the document, then key in this number. Save again.

EXERCISE WP 1.1

Recall the report stored as TERM. Amend as shown. Adjust the left margin to 3 cm. Use full justification. Save as REPORT and print one copy.

END OF TERM REPORT

this paragraph only in double linespacing

Most of the students on the audio/legal typing course have worked hard this term and have reached the required standards. The department head and the class teacher held meetings with each student during the final week of term. Progress to date was discussed as well as any concerns the student had about their course work.

the first week of

Some members of the class said that they would like more English lessons. It has therefore been decided to begin classes on a Tuesday morning at 9.30am instead of 10.30am. This hour will be an English lesson. The early start on Tuesdays will take effect from next term.

The programme for weekly tests was distributed. Details of the pass marks and the final examination at the end of next term were given to the students.

Move to point marked A

All the students are very happy and eager to complete their final term so that they can start on their chosen careers.

Kay Potter was ill last term. *Although she was sent work to do at home she has been unable to keep up with the rest of the group. Therefore it has been decided that she should withdraw from this course and join the next course which is due to commence in September. We understand from her parents that she is making a good recovery. Most members of the class have sent her cards.*

Inset this paragraph 2 cm from left margin

Complete homework

The need to ~~finish assignments~~ on time was stressed. There are two class members who are falling behind the rest of the group.

extra

These two were given ~~additional~~ homework to complete during the holiday. ✓

Ⓐ

On completion, ensure you have saved your work and then use your software facilities to perform a word count. Key in this figure on a separate line below the final line of text.

Insert an automatic filename and path in the footer area

EXERCISE WP 1.2

Recall the article stored as RISK. Amend as shown. Adjust the left margin to 5cm. Use full justification. Save as INSURE and print one copy.

MINIMISING RISK

Daily life can be dangerous. Many of the actions have an associated risk. Some people are happy to accept that risk. Others prefer to take out insurance to cover themselves against accidents and hazards. At Progress Insurance we have a range of policies to cover most of life's dangers. Premiums are low and can be [further] [reduced] by accepting an excess which is payable on any claims made.

we take

If you would like a personalised quotation on any of our policies, contact Progress Insurance now on 024 7647 0033. We look forward to receiving your call.

move to point marked ⊙

This paragraph only in double linespacing

One of the most important insurances that ~~householders~~ homeowners can take out is house and contents cover. This insures the policyholder against damage to a dwelling and its contents. Should the property be burgled or damaged, a claim can be made to replace the items affected. Many people underestimate the value of their furnishings, so it is very important to review the figure on a regular basis.

⊘

inset this paragraph 3cm from left margin

Car drivers will understand the importance of motor insurance. Comprehensive insurance covers the driver and any car driven. Third party insurance covers the policyholder only against damage caused to the other person and vehicle. People who drive inexpensive vehicles often opt for this policy because the annual charge is much cheaper.

Travel insurance
~~Overseas cover~~ is another safeguard that is offered to the general public. Single trip or annual cover will protect the traveller against delays, cancellations and loss of luggage or money.

Although this insurance is a sensible precaution, many people think it is too expensive and are willing to take the risk when travelling.

⊙

On completion, ensure you have saved your work and then use your software facilities to perform a word count. Key in this figure on a separate line below the final line of text.

Insert an automatic filename and path in the footer area

EXERCISE WP 1.3

Recall the article stored as INDUCTION. Amend as shown. Adjust the left margin to 3cm. Use full justification. Save as INDUCTION 2 and print one copy.

INDUCTION PROCEDURE

with an interactive program

A new induction procedure is being drawn up. The responsibility for delivering the majority of the induction is being transferred to departments.

Human Resources will still have overall responsibility and will provide guidelines. The aim is to give information in several ways and not to overload the new recruit with too much information. Interactive programs are being used. These have the advantage that the new employee can go through them several times at a steady pace.

Ⓐ

Information from Personnel will now be done online and includes several online quizzes.

☑ The building ~~tour~~ visit should not be restricted just to where the new employee will be working. It is suggested that this is done during the first day. It should provide a useful guide to the whole building.

This paragraph only in double linespacing

done with an interactive program

The health and safety briefing will be ~~online using the computer~~. This will give a good overview of the important points. Line managers must go through specific points relating to the recruit's job.

Move to point marked Ⓐ

There will be a central induction of a full day, which will take place every 6 weeks, to which all new employees will be invited.

Inset this paragraph 2cm from left margin

Line managers must ensure that the new employee understands the job role and how it links in to the business as a whole. We are introducing a "buddy" system. Line managers will need to allocate a colleague, who is not the line manager, to mentor the recruit. The aim is to provide a point of contact for any routine queries.

Please let us have any ideas to improve the procedure.

On completion, ensure you have saved your work and then use your software facilities to perform a word count. Key in this figure on a separate line below the final line of text.

Insert an automatic filename and path in the footer area.

POSTER/ADVERTISEMENT/NOTICE

Amendments to text

Refer to page 18 for the Word Processing Syllabus in the 'Assessment Criteria' section showing the list of amendment and correction signs. Some of these will appear in the display exercises.

Insert a full-page border

To do this use **Format** ➤ **Borders and Shading** ➤ **Page Border** ➤ click on **Box** ➤ check that *Apply to whole document* is showing.

Insert a picture

You will be told to insert a picture in the document. At this level you are not required to change the measurement of the picture or to wrap the text round it. However, you must place the picture in the vertical position indicated in the draft, but it may be positioned anywhere across the page. You may use any picture you choose, but a selection has been provided on the Hodder Plus website should you prefer to use this. The filenames are:

BEACH HUTS	BUILDING	OFFICE
PEONY	PREMISES	PROGRESS

Underline text

You will be required to underline several words as shown on the draft. Make sure that the underlining does not extend either side of the selected words, although it may include any punctuation that is part of the word. The examples on page 59 show acceptable styles of underlining.

Emphasis

You will be instructed to emphasise a portion of text. You may use bold, italics, underlining or change of font style/size. Make sure that you emphasise only the section indicated.

Centre

You will be instructed to centre one portion of text. Select the text you wish to centre, then click on the **Align Center** icon above the top ruler line. Make sure that you return to left-aligned text once you have completed that section, by clicking on the **Align Left** icon above the top ruler line.

EXERCISE WP 1.4

Recall the advert stored as ADVERT. Amend as shown. Save as COURSES and print one copy.

SECRETARIAL AND BUSINESS STUDIES COURSES ← (centre this heading)

At the end of last term the ~~secretarial and business studies~~ building was modernised.

(Insert a picture here)

                                                    and chairs
The canteen has been refitted and new tables have been purchased.

All classrooms have new computers and printers.

Enrol by the end of this month for the following courses:

Getting the best from your computer
Medical typing
Word processing
Touch typing
Speed keying
Legal typing

(Emphasise this sentence)

Course teachers will be happy to talk with prospective students in order to offer advice.

There is no need to make an appointment.

There will be teachers available on Monday and Tuesday mornings until the end of the month.

For a guided tour of the new building please ask at the main reception.

(Insert a full-page border)

EXERCISE WP 1.5

> Recall the advert stored as COLLEGE. Amend as shown. Save as COURSES and print one copy.

PHOTOGRAPHY COURSES AT PROGRESS COLLEGE

> Insert a picture here

to take
Do you like/photographs? Are you disappointed with the results? Would you like to learn new techniques ~~and improve your skill~~?

If the answer to any of the above questions is yes, why not consider enrolling on a photography course at Progress College? Next term we have a wide range of courses on offer.

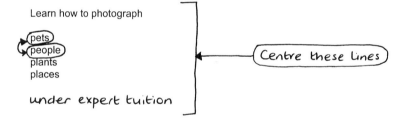

Learn how to photograph

pets
people
plants
places

> Centre these lines

under expert tuition

Our spacious photographic studios offer first-class facilities. Courses are held during the day and in the evening. <u>We even run a Saturday class.</u>

> Emphasise this sentence

Come along to our Open Day next month. Our tutors will be there to answer your questions.

> Insert a full-page border

EXERCISE WP 1.6

Recall the advertisement stored as OFFICE. Amend as shown. Save as OFFICE2 and print one copy.

OFFICE EQUIPMENT EXHIBITION   *Emphasise this sentence*

suitable

There will be an exhibition of a range of equipment/for the small office or for the home.

Next Wednesday in the Town Hall Chambers from 10.00 am to 8.00 pm.

Come along to see the latest equipment.

Insert a picture here

Over 20 exhibitors have taken stands and there will be demonstrations running throughout the day. It is a good opportunity to ask questions.

Stands include

Colour printers
Small, easy to use photocopiers
Desks and chairs   *Centre these lines*
Laptops and notebooks
Binders and laminators
Telephones

There are also stands giving good prices on a wide range of stationery and other items.

Have a free cup of coffee with this advertisement.

Insert a full-page border

DOCUMENT WITH TABLE

Tables versus tabs

In a simple, straightforward display of columns, it is possible to use preset tabs or tabs that you have set yourself. However, where you have to rearrange text, it is easier to use the tables facility.

In this document it is recommended that you use the tables method, as you are instructed to alter the order of the text. You will find it simpler to key in the table as it is drafted and then modify the layout as instructed, using the tables facility.

Column width and spacing between

Using the table method, it is simple to insert a table. Choose the number of columns you need and keep the automatic column width. Use **Table ➤ Insert Table ➤** against *Number of columns* select **3 ➤** leave *Number of rows* at **2 ➤** *Fixed column width* should show **Auto**.

When keying in, let the text wrap round inside the cells, moving between them using the tab or cursor keys. To create more rows, make sure the cursor is in the last cell and press the tab key.

The spacing between each column does not have to be the same. However, if you wish to alter the column widths, you can do this by placing your cursor on the line between each column and dragging it to the left or right.

There should be a clear linespace between the headings and the first row of text.

Modify layout

Make sure your cursor is in the correct position in the table for you to make the alteration. Use the table method **Table ➤ Select ➤ Column** or **Select ➤ Row** then click on the **Cut** and **Paste** icons to insert the relevant text in its new position. This should not prove difficult as long as you have left sufficient space in which to paste the selected text. To create space use **Table ➤ Insert ➤ Rows Above/Below** or **Columns to the Left/Columns to the Right** as appropriate.

Rule the table

You will not be penalised if you show ruling. However, if you decide to use grid-lines, you must not leave empty cells or blank rows, as this would incur a penalty. If you wish to remove the ruling before printing, mark the table using **Table ➤ Select ➤ Table** then use **Format ➤ Borders and Shading ➤ Borders ➤** select **None**.

Capitalisation

Follow the draft regarding initial capitals and closed capitals throughout the document, and particularly within the table.

Recalled text

Make sure that you key in any additions to the recall text before the table.

EXERCISE WP 1.7

Recall this document stored as FIRE. Amend as shown. You may include lines of ruling in the table if you wish. Save as MARSHALS and print one copy.

FIRE MARSHALS

The safety of all employees is of paramount importance. For this reason we will undertake a practice evacuation of the building one day next week. Each department has its own fire marshal who will be responsible for all staff leaving the building in an orderly manner.

Employees are requested to familiarise themselves with the fire escape routes, evacuation procedures and assembly points. In order to ensure that everyone is out of the building each floor has been given a unique assembly point which is in the courtyard outside the main entrance.

Names and extension numbers of all the departmental fire marshals are given below.

Display the EXTENSION column after the DEPARTMENT column, eg

FIRE MARSHAL	DEPARTMENT	EXTENSION
Andrew Newcombe	General Office	908

FIRE MARSHAL	EXTENSION	DEPARTMENT
Andrew Newcombe	908	General Office
Paula Tang	145	Marketing and sales
Lucy Cole	768	Payroll and accounts
Anne Gibson	954	Photocopying
Daniel Collins	723	Advertising
Victoria Jones	879	Warehouse and stock
Meena Poole	409	Publishing
Brenda Patel	378	Personnel
Diane Hopwood	975	Reception
Karen Wong	287	Services
Mary Gilbert	705	Canteen and catering
Julie Perry	412	Training and development
Colin Hogan	531	Quality Control
James Laws	691	Stationery and supplies

EXERCISE WP 1.8

> Recall this document stored as STATIONERY. Amend as shown. You may include lines of ruling in the table if you wish. Save as SUPPLIES and print one copy.

PROGRESS STATIONERY SUPPLIES

All our products can be purchased via our website. Alternatively our Customer Service Team will be happy to take your order. We aim to deliver within 4 working days.

Send us a copy of your logo and we can print it on any of our products. In this way you can coordinate your stationery for a truly professional look. When placing your order, please ensure that you indicate clearly the colour and quantity required.

Contact us now to see how you can benefit from a 20% discount on your first order.

Here is a list of our most popular lines this month.

> Display the PACK SIZE column after the DESCRIPTION column, eg
>
> | ITEM | DESCRIPTION | PACK SIZE |
> | --- | --- | --- |
> | Business cards | Premium business cards in silver case | 250 |

ITEM	PACK SIZE	DESCRIPTION
Business cards	250	Premium business cards in silver case
Letterhead	100	A4 letterhead on 90 gsm paper
Envelopes	50	DL envelopes to match letterhead
Return address labels	150	Sticky labels incorporating logo
Folded notecards	50	Personalised notecards with logo
Postcards	100	A6 blank cards
Compliments slips	100	Printed with your details
Rubber stamp	1	Self inking stamp with logo
Tee shirt	1	Cotton tee shirt with logo on pocket

EXERCISE WP 1.9

Recall the document stored as PERMIT. Amend as shown.
You may include lines of ruling in the table if you wish.
Save as PERMIT2 and print one copy.

CAR PERMIT NUMBER CHANGES

Some staff are being given a new car permit number. This is to incorporate the members of staff coming from the Newhall office. The members of staff listed have new numbers. New discs need to be collected from Michelle Dyer in the General Office. Her extension number is 3498.

All members of staff must display their car permit disc on their windscreen. Failure to do this may result in the use of the permit being taken away.

Display the CAR PERMIT column after the JOB TITLE column eg

NAME	JOB TITLE	CAR PERMIT
Allen Greta	Creche Supervisor	267

CAR PERMIT	NAME	JOB TITLE
267	Allen Greta	Creche Supervisor
222	Andrew Harris	Communications Officer
398	Boothe Sharon	Cash Office Assistant
220	Connelly Kevin	Training Co-ordinator
342	Desforges Jen	Help Desk Supervisor
268	Fernandez Marco	Sales Assistant
267	Flint Mavis	Nursery Worker
290	Heath Sara Jane	Marketing Sales Manager
351	Hill Bill	Building Services Officer
397	Jones Katie Anne	Payroll Officer
340	Khan Zafar	Help Desk Assistant
265	Maseuleo Annette	Sales Assistant Manager
292	Oder Peter	Purchase Manager
334	Patel Maz	Telephone Sales Manager
321	Potter Anna Maria	Canteen Manager
341	Wilkinson John	Chief Receptionist
285	Williams Sian	Information Assistant

FORM FOR COMPLETION

Pre-stored form

You are instructed to recall and complete a pre-stored form using the information given in the exercise. The information will be in the same order as that required on the form.

Complete the form

Key in the information against the appropriate headings. Follow the capitalisation given in the draft.

Deletion

There will be two asterisked alternatives with the instruction to *Delete as appropriate using strikethrough.* To do this, select the words you wish to delete, then use **Format** ➤ **Font** ➤ select **Strikethrough**. The text you have chosen will appear in the *Preview* panel, showing the strikethrough.

Make sure you strikethrough only the required text and that it does not go through any of the other words.

Date

The form should be dated with the date that you are doing the exercise.

EXERCISE WP 1.10

Recall the form stored as RETURNS. Complete the form from the information given below. Save as WILSONJ and print one copy.

FULL NAME OF CUSTOMER — Mrs Jane Wilson

HOME ADDRESS — 71 Old Oak Road
Belvedere
Kent
DA17 1NR

DAYTIME TELEPHONE NUMBER — 020 7461 4063

EVENING TELEPHONE NUMBER — 020 7461 4064

ORDER NUMBER — 2160

REASON FOR RETURN — Arrived too late for the birthday party

CODE	DEPARTMENT	DESCRIPTION
50A	Paper goods	Red disposable drinking cups
30B	Decorations	Balloons and paper chains
10C	Paper goods	Blue floral patterned plates
40E	Household linens	Square plastic table cloths
20F	Paper goods	Red and blue napkins
10H	Decorations	Silk flowers for table centres

Please arrange for a refund for the customer

EXERCISE WP 1.11

Recall the form stored as GROUP. Complete the form from the information given below. Save as COOKERY and print one copy.

PROVIDER	Progress Cookery School
VENUE	Redruth House Longtown Road Banbury OX4 8TV
TELEPHONE NUMBER	01632 960537
GROUP LEADER	Ms Gemma Wilkinson
ADDRESS	46 Mountsorrel Road Leamington Spa CV31 2GX
CONTACT NUMBER	07776 387662
EMAIL ADDRESS	gemmaw@quickchat.co.uk
NAMES OF GROUP MEMBERS	Miss Maddie Turner Mrs Judy Greville Mrs Sally de Souza Ms Hanna Blake Mrs Tina Doyle

COURSE	LEVEL	COST
Sharpen Those Knife Skills	Elementary	£140
Italian Desserts and Biscuits	Intermediate	£165
A Perfect Summer Supper Party	Intermediate	£200
Passionate about Patisserie	Advanced	£220

Group leader is entitled to one free place

EXERCISE WP 1.12

Recall the form stored as COURSES. Complete the form from the information given below. Save as COURSES2 and print one copy.

NAME

JOB ROLE

HOME ADDRESS

Joe Wood
Assistant Sales Manager

Flat 2
34 Trent Lane
HARROGATE
HG1 5TP

TELEPHONE NUMBER

FAX NUMBER

0163 296 0457

0163 296 4680

TITLE OF COURSE	LOCATION	LENGTH (NUMBER OF DAYS, WEEKS)
Introduction to Presentation Skills	Wakefield	2 days
Client Care (Part 1)	Leeds	3 days
Child Protection	Head Office	1 day
Induction to the Company	Head Office	1 day
Telephone Skills	Manchester	2 days
Advanced Selling Methods	Training Centre	18 weeks
Team Building (Part 2)	Chester	1 week

Manager's approval has been given.

AUDIO-TRANSCRIPTION LEVEL 1 PRACTICE EXERCISES

WITH DETAILED NOTES ON HOW TO WORK THE FOLLOWING DOCUMENTS:

- Letter
- Memo
- Notice
- Report
- Article

LETTER

See the notes under Text Production (page 37) for details on layout of business letters. Unless stated otherwise, the same rules apply to Audio-Transcription.

Candidate Information Sheet

The Candidate Information Sheet provided in this section contains references, names, addresses and proper nouns. This is to help you with the spelling of such words.

Reference

Key in the reference exactly as shown on the reference sheet with regard to spacing, punctuation and capitalisation. Do not add your initials to a reference, or add a *Your ref*, as this will incur a penalty.

Date

You must date this document with the date on which you work it. See the detailed notes under Text Production (page 38).

Heading

Follow capitalisation and underlining as dictated.

Punctuation

All essential punctuation is dictated, except for the end of a paragraph, when the word *paragraph* will indicate a final full stop followed by a clear linespace.

Enclosure

You will be required to show an enclosure as indicated in the dictation. Follow the instructions given for business letter layout in the Text Production notes (page 39).

Accessing audio exercises material

Candidate Information Sheets

Candidate Information Sheets follow for exercises:

- AT 1.1
- AT 1.2
- AT 1.3

Templates

The letter template is available on the Hodder Plus website at **www. hodderplus.co.uk/ocrtextprocessing**. The same template can be used for all exercises.

Dictated documents

The dictation for the above exercises is available on the Hodder Plus website.

EXERCISE AT 1.1

CANDIDATE INFORMATION SHEET

Included in dictation:

Aruna Dipak
Boutique Asianna
Tanvir Kabir
Senior Accountant

Address:

Swan Cottage
Mill Pond Lane
Mickle Trafford
CHESTER
CH3 7MD

Reference(s):

TK/QK

NB: All other instructions (eg courtesy titles, headings, etc) will be given in the dictation.

EXERCISE AT 1.2

CANDIDATE INFORMATION SHEET

Included in dictation:

Lorraine Finlayson
Linda Hardwick
Colin Bacchus
Manager

References:

CB/PT

Address:

193 Station Road
COLWYN BAY
LL28 9XT

NB: All other instructions (eg courtesy titles, department names, headings etc) will
be given in the dictation.

EXERCISE AT 1.3

CANDIDATE INFORMATION SHEET

Included in dictation:

Trevor Cousins
Julia Webb
Customer Service Manager

References:

JW/AD

Address:

38 Western Park Avenue
HAPTON
Norfolk
NR31 6WG

NB: All other instructions (eg courtesy titles, department names, headings etc) will be given in the dictation.

MEMO/NOTICE

Layout and style

The memo and notice documents should be produced on plain A4 paper. OCR templates are provided for memo documents. Add the details provided in the dictation against the relevant headings. It is particularly important to check that the *To* and *From* details in the memo are against the correct headings, as they are not always drafted in the same order. The following styles are acceptable: leaving equal spaces; leaving unequal spaces; using a tab stop.

Use the mouse or cursor keys to move between headings, to avoid creating extra linespaces. Do not add punctuation after the headings or infill details.

Reference

You must insert a reference in a memo. Key in the reference as shown on the Candidate Information Sheet regarding spacing, punctuation and capitalisation. Do not add your initials to a reference, or add a *Your ref*, as this will incur a penalty.

You must not add a reference to a notice.

Date

You must date a memo with the date on which you work it. Acceptable styles are given in the Text Production notes for business letters (page 38).

You should not date a notice, as this would incur a penalty.

Heading

You will be instructed to insert a heading. Follow capitalisation as dictated.

Punctuation

All essential punctuation is dictated, except for the end of a paragraph, when the word *paragraph* will indicate a final full stop followed by a clear linespace.

Accessing audio exercises material

Candidate Information Sheets

Candidate Information Sheets follow for exercises:

- AT 1.4
- AT 1.5
- AT 1.6
- AT 1.7
- AT 1.8
- AT 1.9

Templates

The memo template is available on the Hodder Plus website at **www. hodderplus.co.uk/ocrtextprocessing**. The same template can be used for all exercises.

Dictated documents

The dictation for the above exercises is available on the Hodder Plus website.

EXERCISE AT 1.4

CANDIDATE INFORMATION SHEET

Included in dictation:

Marcus Osbert
Service Manager
Ciaran Doherty
Customer Liaison Department
Prowess Astute
Lady Vixen

Addresses:

Reference(s):

MO/WP

NB: All other instructions (eg courtesy titles, headings, etc) will be given in the dictation.

EXERCISE AT 1.5

CANDIDATE INFORMATION SHEET

Included in dictation:

Clerk to the Council
All Parish Councillors

References:

MDG/DH

Address:

NB: All other instructions (eg courtesy titles, department names, headings etc) will
        be given in the dictation.

EXERCISE AT 1.6

CANDIDATE INFORMATION SHEET

Included in dictation:

Jo Daniels
Alistair McEvoy
Junior Secretary

References:

AM/DH

Address:

NB: All other instructions (eg courtesy titles, department names, headings etc) will be given in the dictation.

EXERCISE AT 1.7

CANDIDATE INFORMATION SHEET

Included in dictation:

PA
Sable

Addresses:

Reference(s):

NB: All other instructions (eg courtesy titles, headings, etc) will be given in the dictation.

EXERCISE AT 1.8

CANDIDATE INFORMATION SHEET

Included in dictation:

Parish Rooms
Parish Clerk

References:

Address:

NB: All other instructions (eg courtesy titles, department names, headings etc) will
be given in the dictation.

EXERCISE AT 1.9

CANDIDATE INFORMATION SHEET

Included in dictation:

Organic Farm Foods
Ipswich

References:

Address:

NB: All other instructions (eg courtesy titles, department names, headings etc) will be given in the dictation.

REPORT/ARTICLE

Heading

You will be instructed to insert a heading. Follow capitalisation as dictated.

Punctuation

All essential punctuation is dictated, except for the end of a paragraph, when the word *paragraph* will indicate a final full stop followed by a clear linespace.

Linespacing

You will be instructed to change the linespacing of a section of text. At the beginning of the section you will hear *Operator: please change to … line-spacing for the following paragraph.* At the end of that section you will be told *Operator: that is the end of the paragraph in … linespacing.* Immediately you hear that instruction, return to the original linespacing for the rest of the document.

Emphasis

You will be instructed to emphasise a line, sentence or short paragraph. Emboldening, closed capitals, underlining, centring or insetting are all acceptable. Ensure that you turn the emphasis instruction off at the end of the relevant portion of text.

Accessing audio exercises material

Candidate Information Sheets

Candidate Information Sheets follow for exercises:

- AT 1.10
- AT 1.11
- AT 1.12

Dictated documents

The dictation for the above exercises is available on the Hodder Plus website at **www.hodderplus.co.uk/ocrtextprocessing**.

EXERCISE AT 1.10

CANDIDATE INFORMATION SHEET

Included in dictation:

CV

Addresses:

Reference(s):

NB: All other instructions (eg courtesy titles, headings, etc) will be given in the dictation.

EXERCISE AT 1.11

CANDIDATE INFORMATION SHEET

Included in dictation:

References:

Address:

NB: All other instructions (eg courtesy titles, department names, headings etc) will
        be given in the dictation.

EXERCISE AT 1.12

CANDIDATE INFORMATION SHEET

Included in dictation:

Progress Friendly Society

References:

Address:

NB: All other instructions (eg courtesy titles, department names, headings etc) will be given in the dictation.

EXAM WORK

This section provides hints for exam work, together with three new practice exams for each unit, similar to the OCR standard. The hints and complete exams for each different unit are grouped together.

Hints pages

Hints pages precede each set of exams. They remind you of the skills you will have acquired in the practice exercises and of the methods you can use to successfully complete each exam. Take the time to read the hints relating to each unit before attempting the exam in that subject. You can refer to the hints as you work through each practice exam. *Of course, you may not refer to the notes or hints in this book at the time of sitting the real exams.*

Practice exams

There are three new complete practice exams for each unit. Recall text for these exams is available on the Hodder Plus website (see below). Once you have finished a complete exam, proofread it and correct any errors. Make sure you have saved the final version of each document, using the filenames indicated, and print copies. Find the correct worked example of the exam in the 'Worked Examples' section and proofread your copy against this. If you are a member of a group, you may find it helpful to proofread each other's work, or your tutor may wish to take in your work for marking.

Recall text from the Hodder Plus website

You will need to access files on the Hodder Plus website at **www.hodderplus.co.uk/ocrtextprocessing** in order to carry out the following:

- open and use letterhead and memo templates
- recall text and amend as instructed
- access dictation for the audio-transcription exams

The templates that you will need to recall are saved under the following filenames:

LETTERHEAD   MEMO

For the purpose of these practice exams, you may use the same letterhead for any of the Text Production or Audio-Transcription documents, although some of the worked examples may show different letterheads. Under actual exam conditions you must use the templates provided for that particular paper. The same applies to other templates, where slight variations may occur.

The recall text for Word Processing is saved under the filenames given in each document in the practice exams.

Audio-Transcription

The Candidate Information Sheets (containing proper nouns) are provided in this section. Dictated material is saved under the filenames given to each document and is accessed from the Hodder Plus website at **www. hodderplus.co.uk/ocrtextprocessing**.

TEXT PRODUCTION LEVEL 1 PRACTICE EXAMS

WITH HINTS SHEETS COVERING

- Skills Checklist
- General Hints
- Hints for Each Document

HINTS FOR EXAM WORK: OCR TEXT PRODUCTION LEVEL 1

Checklist of skills

You need to be able to carry out the following before you attempt the practice exams:

- recall and use a letterhead
- lay out a letter
- lay out a menu/notice/advertisement
- alter linespacing
- emphasise and underline text and headings
- create new paragraphs
- interpret and carry out amendment and correction signs
- expand abbreviations from OCR list
- spell words from OCR list of business vocabulary
- correct identified grammatical and apostrophe errors
- correct identified typographical, spelling and punctuation errors
- incorporate information from a resource sheet
- indicate enclosure(s).

General

- Start a **New** file for each document.
- It is good practice to use either the **Header** or **Footer** facility to record your name, centre number and document number (together with automatic page numbering on any multi-paged document) on each printout.
- Recall a letterhead and use **Save As** to give it a filename.
- Thereafter click on the **Save** screen icon frequently as you work.
- As a general rule for these exam units, carry out editing instructions as you key in, apart from linespacing instructions, which can be left to the end.
- When sitting a real exam, as you complete each instruction tick it off on the question paper. This makes it easier to keep track, particularly when working on a multi-paged document. It may not be appropriate to mark the textbook, unless it is your own property.
- As you key in an email or internet address, your computer changes the text colour to blue and underscores it. It can be left like this.
- You may print as often as you wish, both during and immediately after the exam time allocation. However, remember that the process is time-consuming, particularly when many candidates are involved, so you should proofread carefully from the screen prior to printing.
- Proofread a second time from the hard copy.
- **Ensure you have SAVED your final edited version of each document before you log off at the end of the session.**

Document 1: letter

- You must use the OCR letterhead provided for your examination.
- It must be dated with the date you are doing the practice exam.
- Key in any reference exactly as shown. Only insert a *Your ref* if one is given. Do not add your own initials.
- Key in text, making amendments according to the draft.
- Follow draft for capitalisation.
- Correct circled spelling and punctuation errors, including apostrophes.
- Abbreviations, which are not circled, should be identified by you and expanded. (See details in the Letter Notes section, pages 37–41.)
- When underlining text, ensure that the line does not overshoot either end of the relevant text. It may include any punctuation that is part of the final word.
- Find a word in the Resource Sheet to finish an incomplete word drafted in this document, such as *65 A____ Crescent.*

- The letter is designed to fit on to one page. Single-page documents should not be numbered, but if your letter extends to a second page then the continuation sheets must be numbered. Use **Insert → Page Numbers** to customise your numbering.
- Remember to indicate any enclosure(s) mentioned in the body of the letter.
- Proofread carefully, use the **Spellcheck**, and check that you have not omitted or misplaced text.

Document 2: menu/notice/advertisement

- Key in text, making amendments according to the draft as you work.
- Follow draft for capitalisation.
- Correct circled spelling errors.
- Correct circled apostrophe errors.
- Abbreviations, which are not circled, should be identified by you and expanded. (See details in the Letter Notes section, page 48.)

Document 3: report or article

- Key in text, making amendments according to the draft.
- Linespacing alterations may be left to the end.
- Follow draft for capitalisation.
- Correct circled typographical and spelling errors.
- Correct circled grammatical errors.
- Abbreviations, which are not circled, should be identified by you and expanded. (See details in the Letter Notes section.)
- When emphasising a portion of text, ensure that only the indicated portion is emphasised. This is usually carried out by emboldening or using closed capitals.
- When underlining text, ensure that the line does not overshoot either end of the relevant text. It may include any punctuation that is part of the final word.
- If the document runs to more than a single page, the continuation sheet must be numbered. Use **Insert → Page Numbers** to customise your numbering. Single sheets should not be numbered.
- Proofread carefully, use the **Spellcheck**, and check that you have not omitted or misplaced text.

EXAM TP 1.A1

Our ref BK/EH

Mrs J Devon
64 Orchard Cres
WELLINGTON
Somerset
TA21 1PR

Dr Mrs Devon

Thank you for your recent letter about the post of audio typist. I enclose an application form which you should complete. Please return this to me by Fri next week. If you are chosen to attend for an interview I will contact you again. The selection process will include an English test and an audio typing test. I need to be sure that your English skills are very good and that you are a fast typist.

The typing section is based in our T____ office. We need to employ six more typists to work in this office. One of our major cleints has asked if we can complete some extra work for them. In order for us to be able to do this work we have to employ more staff.

I look forward to receiving copies of your examination certificates and your application form. Please contact me if you have any questions.

If you do not hear from me ~~within during~~ the next ✓ two week's you may assume that your application has not been a success.

Yours sncly

Bethany Kane
Production Manager

Enc

RESOURCE SHEET

DOCUMENT 1

The typing section is based in our Taunton office.

EXAM TP 1.A2

PROGRESS SHOE SHOP

Please note that we are moving to a larger *(is next door and)* shop very soon.

The new shop was, until the end of last year, a bank.

We will be able to stock a wide range of walking and climbing boots.

After we move we will have (suficient) space for a new department.

Please ask a member of staff if you would like ~~us to send you~~ further details about the new shop.

(Emphasise this sentence)

There will be many special discounts during the first week.

We look forward to your continued custom.

EXAM TP 1.B1

(Use single linespacing except where indicated)

SAVING AND INVESTMENTS WITH PROGRESS BANK

There are many reasons why you should open a savings account with this bank. We offer our customers a wide range of investment opps.

You may want your money to be safe or you may be happy to take some small risks. We can provide you with either type of saving plan.

(This paragraph only in double linespacing)

Our experiensed staff will be pleased to discuss our saving plans with you. Perhaps you would like a savings account with eas6y access or you may be happy to invest your money for three years or more. Whatever your needs are we have a savings plan that will suit you.

very easy when you bank with Progress

Opening an account is simple if you already are a customer. There is a simple form to complet before we can process your application. This form can be completed in your local branch or on our web site. New customers can only open an account by going to their local branch. We will need to check your identity if you do not bank currently with us. We have a legal duty to confirm who you are and where you live. This applies to each person when accounts are opened in joint names. New customres also need to provide two sample of their signature. We keep alll these signatures. They are referred to by bank staff when money is withdrawn from the bank.

an appointment

If you would like to discuss your savings please tel us or call into your local branch.

EXAM TP 1.B1

Our Ref   MF/36

Mrs Julia McDade
14 Windsor Ave
STEVENAGE
SG7 4XP

Dear Mrs McDade

Thank you for calling at the office last week. It was very ~~useful~~ ~~helpful~~ to be able to discuss your exact requirements in greater detail. Please confirm that you plan to invite 30 guests to your husbands' birthday lunch.

I have had an opp to prepare a quotation. I hope you will find it acceptable. The cost of our luxury buffet for 30 people will be £450 plus VAT. A ten per cent deposit will be required.

Our luxury buffet option comprises four seperate meat and fish platters plus a selection of quiches and salads. These are followed by small dishes of strawberries and cream along with a range of other desserts and fresh fruit.

All the items are attractively presented on silver serving dishes. The sizing of the portions ensures that guests can remain standing whilst they enjoy their lunch.

Soft drinks and j—— are included in the price. Wines are available at extra cost. I enclose a copy of our brochure which gives detailed info about our buffets. I look forward to hearing from you

Yours sncly

Martina Felton
Managing Director

Enc

RESOURCE SHEET

Soft drinks and juices are included in the price of the menus.

EXAM TP 1.B2

Children's Parties ← (emphasise this heading)

Progress Party Foods can supply ▼food for any occasion. Parties, in particular, are our speciality.

This month we launch a new children's party line.

We are always happy to discuss your personal menu choices.

(a wide variety of)

The delicious menu includes

Pirate ship platter

Savoury bites

Fruit salad selection

Organic gingerbread men

Chocolate pirate ship cake

Each menu is (suficient) to feed twelve hungry children. The cost is ~~a bargain at only~~ £5 per head plus delivery. We also supply healthy lunch boxes for children on the move.

Call us now!

EXAM TP 1.B3

PROGRESS PARTY FOODS

A TASTE OF EXCELLENCE

Use double linespacing except where indicated

Whatever the occasion, Progress Party Foods can provide ~~you with~~ perfect food choices to suit ~~all~~ your guests. Our co has been in the catering ~~bussiness~~ for fifteen yrs and we have earned a reputation for quality and style.

Our menus are designed for all age groups. We cater for children's parties, ~~wedd8ing~~ breakfasts and ~~retirment~~ lunches. We can cook for a dinner party if you wish. In all cases we aim to provide a balance of healthy foods and gourmet delights. We ~~always will~~ suggest <u>healthy options</u>. Please let us know if you or your guests have special dietary needs.

This paragraph only in single linespacing

Our ingredients are sourced locally. Local farmers supply us with top quality produce. Most of our menus ~~reflects~~ seasonal changes. We like to serve food which is at its best.

Our brochure lists our buffet options. You can choose from several themed menus. In all cases, soft drinks and juices are included in the price. Wine can be ordered at additional cost. Alternatively, you may wish to use your own supplier. The choice is yours.

Children's parties are very popular. We offer ~~variuos~~ options, including lunch boxes for children ~~who are spending their day out and about.~~ whose birthday treat involves an excursion with friends

You will be surprised how economical these can be. Prices start at £5 per person plus delivery.

Why not invite us to cater for your next event? We are offering new customers a ten per cent discount. Ring 253761 and request our latest brochure.

EXAM TP 1.C1

Our Ref PW/AY

Mr C Lynch
28 Chapel Sq
WALCOTT
Norfolk
NR12 9VX

Dr Mr Lynch

We are pleased to learn that you have chosen to renew your car insurance with us once again. Your new P————— is enclosed. [We can also provide cover for your home, life and even your pet. Our home insurance includes all buildings. This takes in sheds and items left in the garden overnight. Buying life cover means that your family would be looked after should you die within the term of your contract] If you have a cat or dog, then our pet insurance will save you having to pay out large sums of money for veterinary fees. Older pets are covered too.

In addition, our co can help you manage your finanses. This applies to saving's and credit card payments. Our direct saver a/c is easy to open with as little as £1. Fixed loans are also available. The amount offered will depend on your credit rating. The sum borrowed can be repaid over a set period of time to suit you.

To find out more, please contact the number given on this letterhead.

Yours sincerely

Philip Wainwright
Insurance Adviser

Enc

RESOURCE SHEET

Your new policy is enclosed.

EXAM TP 1.C2

SALES EXECUTIVE

PROGRESS GROUP

We are looking for an experienced and highly motivated person to lead our sales team based in Norfolk.

Good communication skills are required. You must also be able to build up first-class client relations. To succeed in this post you will show a strong desire to achieve our sales targets. Working as a team member is vital.

emphasise this sentence

Please apply in writing with a curriculum vitae to ~~the Human Resource Section~~ Progress Group, Progress House, Westwood Way, Coventry, CV4 8JQ. Interviews will be held early next month.

within the next 2 weeks

EXAM TP 1.C3

Use double linespacing except where indicated

PROGRESS GROUP HOLDS ITS GROUND

BRIEF REPORT TO SHAREHOLDERS

In spite of a troubled year worldwide, the Progress Group has continued to hold its ground. Activities in sales, buildings and marketing all show pleasing results. The org is therefore able to carry on the upward trend of recent years. Group turnover increased by a modest 5% and net sales were also up compared to last year.

All our past hard work has helped us to create a solid base. Our business model has proved itself. However, we canot rest on our laurels. Challenges is always present both inside and outside the group. New s6ystems and processes have to be tested and we must move with the times. Long term social and economic trends must also be taken into accuont.

these paragraphs only in single linespacing

One of our main goals at present is to expand our customer base.

Marketing campaigns are helping to achieve this. ~~Our advertising on television has reaped its benefit.~~ This year, for instance, the sales of our own brand of products have been enhanced greatly by putting large sums of money into advertising.

We are still active in looking after our buildings. In this respect those outlets not reaching their targets are being sold off. The income recieved will be invested in those where potential growth has been forecast.

all aspects of

With the above in mind, the group looks set to achieve good results in its business in the years to come.

We look forward to seeing many of our members at the Annual General Mtg next month.

WORD PROCESSING LEVEL 1 PRACTICE EXAMS

WITH HINTS SHEETS COVERING

- Skills Checklist
- General Hints
- Hints for Each Document

HINTS FOR EXAM WORK: OCR WORD PROCESSING LEVEL 1

Checklist of skills

You need to be able to carry out the following before you attempt the practice exams:

- recall documents
- complete a pre-stored form
- add headers and footers
- insert an automatic filename and path
- change the left margin
- inset, justify and centre text
- alter linespacing of a section of text
- insert a full-page border
- insert a picture
- emphasise and underline text
- interpret amendment and correction signs
- move text by using cut and paste facility
- present information in tables format
- carry out an automatic word count.

General

- Recall a pre-stored document as instructed
- It is good practice to use either the **Header** or **Footer** facility to record your name, centre number and document number on each printout.
- Recall text for these exams is available on the Hodder Plus website at **www.hodderplus.co.uk/ocrtextprocessing**. Use **Save As** to save under the filename indicated.
  Thereafter click on the **Save** icon frequently as you edit the document.
- As a general rule, for these exam units, key in the extra text first and then carry out editing instructions. Leave any linespace editing to the end.

- When sitting a real exam, as you complete each instruction tick it off on the question paper. This makes it easier to keep track, particularly when working on a multi-paged document. However, it may not be appropriate to mark the textbook, unless it is your own property.
- As you key in an email or Internet address, your computer may change the text colour and underscore it. This is acceptable in the exam.
- You may print as often as you wish, both during and immediately after the exam time allocation. However, remember that the process is time-consuming, particularly when many candidates are involved, so you should proofread carefully from the screen prior to printing.
- Proofread a second time from the hard copy.
- **Ensure you have SAVED your final edited version of each document before you log off at the end of the session.**

Document 1: report/article/information sheet

- Recall the stored document as instructed.
- To adjust the left margin use **File** ➤ **Page Setup** or drag it on the ruler (you need to be in *Print Layout View*).
- To justify text, highlight the document and click on the justify icon.
- To insert a **Header** or **Footer** use **View** ➤ **Header and Footer** ➤ select either one ➤ key text in box.
- To insert an automatic filename and path in the footer, use **View** ➤ **Header and Footer** ➤ select **Footer** ➤ click **Insert Auto Text** ➤ select **Filename and Path**. When the data appears, click **Close**, then continue with keying in the rest of the text for the document.
- When you **Move** a section of text it should appear *once* in the document – use the **Cut** and **Paste** icons.
- Proofread carefully, using the **Spellcheck**, and check that you have not omitted or misplaced text.
- Leave the word count until the very end. Save the document, then use **Tools** ➤ **Word Count** and key the number of words specified at the bottom of the document, leaving a clear linespace before it. Save again.

Document 2: notice/poster/advertisement

- Recall the stored document as instructed.
- To insert a full-page border use **Format** ➤ **Borders and Shading** ➤ **Page Border** ➤ click on **Box** ➤ check that *Apply to whole document* is showing and click **OK**.
- Insert a picture of your choice where indicated. You do not have to change the size or wrap text around the picture at this level.

- When underlining a section of text, it may include any punctuation following the final word. Make sure that you take off the instruction at the end of the relevant portion.
- When centring a section of text, highlight the relevant portion and click the **Align Centre** icon. Make sure you return to normal alignment afterwards.
- Proofread carefully, use the **Spellcheck**, and check that you have not omitted or misplaced text.

Document 3: table

- Recall the stored document as instructed.
- This document includes a three-column table.
- It is best to use the tables function for tabular work, to enable you to carry out the editing efficiently.

Displaying tabular work using tables function

- To insert a table use **Table** ➤ **Insert** ➤ **Table** ➤ select 3 **Columns** and 2 **Rows**. Create more rows as required by positioning your cursor in the last cell and pressing the tab key.
- Work in *Page Layout View*.
- Key each line horizontally, and use the tab key or cursor to move between cells.
- Follow draft for capitalisation.
- **Save** your work as soon as you have keyed in all the text. If some of your work is lost when editing the table, you should be able to recall the document at the point that you last saved it.
- Do your initial proofreading before moving or modifying text. It is easier to check against the draft at this stage.
- Column widths can easily be altered by dragging the borders with the mouse.
- Extra line spaces can be inserted at this stage by pressing **Enter** from within the last cell.
- To create space for moving text use **Table** ➤ **Insert** ➤ **Rows Above/Below** or **Columns to the Left/Columns to the Right** as appropriate.
- Use **Table** ➤ **Select Row** or **Select Column** in order to highlight text to be moved, then use **Cut** and **Paste** icons as usual.
- You may print this document with the gridlines showing, but if you prefer not to have them use **Format** ➤ **Borders and Shading** ➤ select **None**.
- Proofread again, checking that headings and columns are aligned consistently, and all modifications and alterations have been completed. Ensure you have included the text before and after the table.

Document 4: form

- Recall a pre-set form using the filename given.
- Date the form with the date that you are sitting the exam.
- The information you need to complete the form is given in logical order on the question sheet. Read through that information first, so that you understand where it has to be keyed.
- To use strikethrough to delete one of the asterisked alternatives, highlight the relevant word(s), then use **Format** ➤ **Font** ➤ select *strikethrough* ➤ click **OK**.

EXAM WP 1.A1

Recall the information sheet stored as MACHINE. Amend as shown. Adjust the left margin to 3cm. Use full justification. Save as SHORTHAND and print one copy.

MACHINE SHORTHAND

Machines have been ~~available~~ used to record the spoken word for many years. ✓ The very first machine was made in 1830 and recorded only symbols on a paper tape.

There have been many changes to the machine since then. Today the symbols are saved to an internal memory.

Inset this paragraph 2 cm from left margin

After the shorthand writer has taken down the spoken word the symbols are then moved to a computer. Then the computer translates this information into text. Until about thirty years ago the symbols would have been read and then typed from the paper tape.

The hours of work vary depending on the type of job and there is not a daily routine. This is an exciting and very rewarding career.

Move to point marked ✳

Trainee shorthand writers

There are a number of training courses. ~~Students on these courses~~ must have a good knowledge of grammar in order to prepare their documents. Some courses include lessons on the English language. //Trainees will be writing at a speed of 180 words per minute at the end of their course. This speed will be adequate to deal with most types of work. Some have passed tests at 300 words per minute.

this paragraph only in double linespacing

This is a very skilled career. There are job opportunities with companies specialising in the supply of transcripts. These companies provide transcripts of court hearings, interviews, tribunals and meetings. The work can be completed very quickly because a computer converts the shorthand into text.

✳ very skilled people

People working in this field travel all over the country and overseas doing a range of work. They meet many interesting people and visit new places during the course of their careers.

On completion, ensure you have saved your work and then use your software facilities to perform a word count. Key in this figure on a separate line below the final line of text.

Insert an automatic filename and path in the footer area.

EXAM WP 1.A2

Recall the poster stored as EXHIBITION. Amend as shown. Save as KITCHEN and print one copy.

EXHIBITION OF KITCHEN EQUIPMENT

Insert a picture here

Town Hall
25 High Street
Chippenham
Wiltshire
SN14 3LT

Telephone   01249   445611

Emphasise this sentence

We will have well-known chefs giving demonstrations.

and equipment

As well as kitchen gadgets there will be a wide range of speciality foods for visitors to purchase. Most stands will have free samples to give away.

The following is a list of some of the items being demonstrated.

Food processors and hand blenders
Ice cream and yoghurt makers
Pressure cookers and steamers
Plastic storage containers

centre these lines

Tickets cost £8 per person on the door, but if you order your tickets in advance you will save £2.

The cafe on the second floor will be open all day and will serve hot and cold refreshments.

Insert a full-page border

EXAM WP 1.A3

Recall this document stored as SITES. Amend as shown. You may include lines of ruling in the table if you wish. Save as HOLIDAY and print one copy.

PROGRESS HOLIDAY SITES

Our holiday sites have excellent facilities and are situated in prime locations. Each site has a general store selling toiletries and groceries, a heated swimming pool and entertainment is provided in the clubhouse during the evenings.

There are many types of accommodation available for visitors. We have a wide range of properties with four bedrooms suitable for large families. There are also smaller properties with one bedroom for couples. All accommodation has a well-equipped kitchen, bath or *shower and a television.*

We have some sites in seaside locations as well as some situated in woodland giving lovely views over surrounding countryside.

Types of property are listed below.

Display the SITE column after the LOCATION column, eg

PROPERTY	LOCATION	SITE
Detached chalets	Devon	10

PROPERTY	SITE	LOCATION
Detached chalets	10	Devon
Mobile homes	12	Cornwall
Thatched cottages	14	Dorset
Studio flats and apartments	16	Somerset
Hostel accommodation	18	Avon
Detached houses	20	Shropshire
Tents and caravans	22	North Yorkshire
Terraced chalets	24	Norfolk
Detached bungalows	26	Kent
Narrow boats and barges	28	West Sussex
Bed and breakfast	30	Essex
Penthouse flats	32	Hampshire
Converted barns	34	Wiltshire
Villas and wooden lodges	36	East Sussex

EXAM WP 1.A4

Recall the form stored as ORDER. Complete the form from the information given below. Save as WATSONR and print one copy.

COMPANY NAME   Progress Group International

COMPANY ADDRESS   Progress House
                        Westwood Way
                        Coventry
                        CV4 8JQ

CONTACT NAME   Mrs Rebecca Watson

TITLE   General Office Manager

TELEPHONE NUMBER   024 7647 0033

FAX NUMBER   024 7646 8080

ACCOUNT NUMBER   4678

DELIVERY INSTRUCTIONS   By overnight courier

QUANTITY	COLOUR	ITEM
10	Black	Bound A4 note books
50 reams	White	A4 copy paper
10 boxes	Brown	Heavy duty envelopes
10	Navy blue	Standard box files
20 packets	Gold	Giant staples
10 boxes	Assorted	Coloured pencils
10	Royal blue	A4 desk diaries

these items are required urgently

EXAM WP 1.B1

Recall the information sheet stored as RECYCLING. Amend as shown. Adjust the left margin to 4 cm. Use full justification. Save as STRATEGY and print one copy.

RECYCLING STRATEGY

In line with Government targets to reduce the amount of waste sent to landfill, Westholme District Council is making recycling as simple as possible for its residents. This year we have managed to reduce the amount of waste sent to landfill by almost 32%, a figure which compares very favourably with other councils in the United Kingdom.

So, what exactly do we do to ~~motivate~~ ~~encourage~~ you to recycle?

Every household is provided with a black wheelie bin, a green bin and a red recycling box. All three containers are collected on a weekly basis. All you have to do is position them at the edge of your property by 0800 on the day specified.

Inset this paragraph 5 cm from left margin

Your recycling box can contain papers, magazines and bottles (plastic). All other household waste should be placed in your black bin. Food and garden waste should be put in the green bin. The contents of this bin will be composted, so it is vital that you do not include other types of waste.

glass and

This paragraph only in double linespacing

(*) Elderly or disabled people who cannot handle their bins can request an assisted collection. The Council will collect the household waste from their door.

Every household is

~~All residents are~~ also entitled to one free collection of three items of bulky material every three months. Bulky material includes items such as fridges, cookers and furniture. Please ensure that you give the Council ten days' notice when you book your collection date.

move to point marked (*)

If you live in a flat you may not have access to individual recycling bins, but there will be communal bins for your building.

On completion, ensure you have saved your work and then use your software facilities to perform a word count. Key in this figure on a separate line below the final line of text.

Insert an automatic filename and path in the footer area

Recall the notice stored as BEACH. Amend as shown. Save as HUTS and print one copy.

BEACH HUTS FOR HIRE ← (Centre this line)

The redevelopment of the South Promenade is now complete. We have opened a new children's playground next to the Pier. In addition, a beach bar and café have started trading.

We have constructed 50 beach huts. These are located on Westholme Chine. They are available for hire, with immediate effect.

Rental charges start at £15 per day.

Daily rental begins at 0800 and ends at 2000.

(Insert a picture here)

Our beach huts at ~~Westholme Chine~~ offer

a café within walking distance
uninterrupted views of the bay
piped drinking water nearby
free local parking

(Emphasise this sentence)

Why not hire a hut this summer? → Give us a call on 01632 960529. We look forward to hearing from you.

(Insert a full-page border)

EXAM WP 1.B3

> Recall this document stored as HIGHWAYS. Amend as shown.
> You may include lines of ruling in the table if you wish. Save as
> WORKS and print one copy.

HIGHWAYS DEPARTMENT – SCHEDULE OF WORK

Within the next few weeks, Westholme District Council staff will be undertaking a number of key projects on roads around the district. Notice is hereby given to the public that the work listed below will commence shortly.

It is likely that temporary traffic lights will have to be installed at some locations to minimise traffic congestion. We will notify local residents in advance of any major disruption. We will also keep our website updated. Please avoid these areas wherever possible.

We apologise for any inconvenience caused by this essential work. Please contact us on 01632 960527 for further information.

> Display the WORK TO BE UNDERTAKEN column after the
> LOCATION column, eg
>
> | LOCATION | WORK TO BE UNDERTAKEN | DURATION (DAYS) |
> | --- | --- | --- |
> | Amberley Road | Re-surface road and pavements | 8 |

WORK TO BE UNDERTAKEN	LOCATION	DURATION (DAYS)
Re-surface road and pavements	Amberley Road	8
Install cycle track	Brierley Gardens	5
Install pelican crossing	Clumber Terrace	4
Replace traffic lights	Finedon Place	5
Upgrade street lighting	Harold Street	2
Install chicanes along route	Kingston Avenue	8
Install additional street lights	Matthew Court	3
Lop and remove overhanging branches	Newton Drive	2
Remove bollards and no entry signs	Parkhurst Square	3
Paint double yellow lines	Selby Road	1

EXAM WP 1.B4

Recall the form stored as MOBILITY. Complete the form from the information given below. Save as ATKINS and print one copy.

NAME OF APPLICANT   Mr Geoffrey William Atkins

ADDRESS   41 Ashley Road
Coombe Park
Westleigh
BN42 5JL

TELEPHONE   01632 960852

DATE OF BIRTH   14 November 1928

NATURE OF DISABILITY   Severe arthritis in joints
Difficulty in walking
Inability to climb stairs

NAME OF ASSESSOR   Jeanette McVitie

CONTACT NUMBERS   Office: 01632 960524
extension 2017
Mobile: 07776 997308

CODE	DESCRIPTION	TIMING
3298	External handrails to front and back doors	Immediate
3241	Indoor walking frame	Immediate
5376	Shower chair	Immediate
6871	Intercom system linked to Councilcare	Within a month

Applicant will require daily help

EXAM WP 1.C1

> Recall the article stored as LAMINATOR. Amend as shown. Adjust the left margin to 4 cm. Use full justification. Save as LAMINATOR2 and print one copy.

LAMINATOR

I have been asked to include, in this newsletter, some tips on how to use the laminator.

> Move to point marked Ⓐ

Staff are very welcome to use the laminator for private use if they buy their own pouches which are available from Kelly Harding.

✓ An A4 laminator has been bought for the ~~staff~~. *office*

It will laminate paper and photographs so will be ideal for laminating notices. A supply of A4, (a packet of 50), and A3, (a packet of 25), pouches has been purchased. A5 and smaller pouches can be bought. Please be careful not to waste pouches as they are very expensive.

> which is important

The pouches are water resistant and can be wiped clean.

Ⓐ
Switch off and unplug the laminator when not in use. Do not use the laminator close to water or spill water on the laminator, the cord or wall socket. Only use the laminator for paper and photographs. This laminator will not do thicker items.

> This paragraph only in double linespacing.

Ensure that the laminator is where there is plenty of space for the pouch to go through easily. Turn the machine on and wait for a green light.

Do a test run before doing anything such as a one-off photograph.

> Inset this paragraph 3cm from left margin.

Always put the item in a pouch. Never laminate an empty pouch. Place the item inside the pouch against the sealed edge. Place pouch, sealed edge first, into the laminator slot. Keep the pouch straight and use the edge guide to centre it.

Immediately remove the item laminated *from the back of the machine* ~~putting it on a clean surface~~. Let the item cool on a flat surface for several seconds before turning it off.

> On completion, ensure you have saved your work and then use your software facilities to perform a word count. Key in this figure on a separate line below the final line of text.

> Insert an automatic filename and path in the footer area.

EXAM WP 1.C2

Recall the advertisement stored as BRIEFINGS.
Amend as shown. Save as BRIEFINGS2 and print one copy.

TECHNICAL BRIEFINGS

It has been agreed that there is a need for [regular technical] briefings. This is in response to several requests from staff who think that email briefings are not working ~~as they should~~.

The meetings will concentrate on any points where demonstrations are useful.

Information will still be sent by email to all staff.

All staff must attend these monthly meetings to keep up to date.

Centre this line

Insert a picture here

Emphasise this sentence

We are hoping to recruit two members of staff to deliver these staff briefings. Training and support will be given. If you are interested please contact Jon Mould on extension 3245. Applicants will be expected to give a short presentation at the interview.

Insert a full-page border

EXAM WP 1.C3

> Recall the document stored as AGENTS. Amend as shown. You may include lines of ruling in the table if you wish. Save as AGENTS 2 and print one copy.

LOCAL AGENTS

The number of clients assigned to each agent varies from month to month. These figures were taken at the beginning of last month. Three agents have only been working for us for 6 months. Their client numbers are low. It takes, on average, a year to build up client numbers.

It is hoped that with increased sales all agents will have a minimum number of 500 clients. At the present time there is no need to recruit any more agents.

> Display the ADDRESS column after the AGENT NAME column eg
>
> | AGENT NAME | ADDRESS | CLIENT NUMBERS |
> |---|---|---|
> | James Harding | Oakdale Square | 567 |

ADDRESS	AGENT NAME	CLIENT NUMBERS
Oakdale Square	James Harding	567
The Walkway	Denise Gumbrill	290
New Road	Peggy Smith	623
Station Mews	Jon Muir	587
Shelley Park Road	Rasool Afzal	555
Broadway Crescent	Margaret Erskine	523
Elm Street	Shahid Iqbal	612
Fir Tree Avenue	Vanessa Chan	573
Pelier Place	Maz Mann	380
Mather Road	June Kohler	590
Grove Road	Kim Betts	602
Ivory Drive	Sally Ann Devine	455
Heather Lea Lane	Maureen Willets	571
Main Crescent	Steve Rocca	633
Ridings Way	Bob Singh	538
Timber Road	Hazel Quinn	570
East Bank Road	Pat McEvoy	505
Naylor Place	Matt Taylor	537

Recall the form stored as DELIVERY. Complete the form from the information given below. Save as DELIVERY2 and print one copy.

TITLE (MR, MRS, MS)	Ms
FIRST NAME(S)	Anne Marie
SURNAME	Baker
HOME ADDRESS	94 Archers Circle Birmingham B15 3EA
TELEPHONE NUMBER	0121 496 5218
ALTERNATIVE DELIVERY ADDRESS	103 Archers Circle Birmingham B15 2EZ
ALTERNATIVE TELEPHONE NUMBER	0121 496 9367

DESCRIPTION OF ITEM	STOCK CODE	NUMBER
A4 packet of white multiuse 90g paper	P34	10
500 sheets of cream card	C23	3
Gloss A4 laminating pouches	L12	4
Box of white laser labels	LL10	2
Pack of manilla self-seal C5 envelopes	E67	10
Laser A4 multipack of 5 colours	P54	2

New customer

AUDIO-TRANSCRIPTION LEVEL 1 PRACTICE EXAMS

WITH HINTS SHEETS COVERING

- Skills Checklist
- General Hints
- Hints for Each Document

HINTS FOR EXAM WORK: OCR AUDIO-TRANSCRIPTION LEVEL 1

Checklist of skills

You need to be able to carry out the following before you attempt the practice exams:

- use the audio equipment provided by your centre
- recall a letterhead and memo template
- lay out a letter
- lay out a memo/notice
- alter linespacing
- emphasise and underline text and headings
- create new paragraphs
- indicate an enclosure.

General

- Start a **New** file for each document.
- It is good to practice to use either the **Header** or **Footer** facility to record your name, centre number and document number on each printout.
- Open and use the letterhead and memo templates as instructed then use **Save As** to give it a filename.
- Click on the **Save** screen icon frequently as you work.
- The dictation for each document is available on the Hodder Plus website.
- Carry out dictated editing instructions as you key in.
- A Candidate Information Sheet is included with each exam. This lists addresses, references and proper nouns. Take care to copy these correctly as the words may be unfamiliar to you.
- When keying in an email or internet address, your computer may change the colour of the text and underscore it. This is acceptable in the exam.
- You may print as often as you wish, both during and immediately after the exam time allocation.

- Once you have completed a document, replay the tape, listening carefully and checking that the hard copy is correct.
- **Ensure you have SAVED your final edited version of each document before you log off at the end of the session.**

Document 1: letter

- This document must be printed on the letterhead template provided.
- It must be dated with the date you are sitting the exam.
- Key in the *Our ref* as dictated. Do not add your own initials or insert a *Your ref*.
- Key in the heading using the capitalisation as dictated.
- Key in the text, making amendments as dictated.
- Follow capitalisation as dictated for text in the body of the letter.
- The letter is designed to fit on to one A4 sheet. Single-page documents should not be numbered, but if your letter extends to a second page then the continuation sheet must be numbered. **Insert ➤ Page Numbers** will allow you to customise your numbering.
- Remember to indicate any enclosure mentioned in the body of the letter by using Enc or Att for single enclosures, or Encs or Atts for multiple enclosures.
- Use the **Spellcheck** and proofread the hard copy carefully, particularly checking you have not omitted or misplaced text.

Document 2: memo/notice

- A memo must be dated with the date you are sitting the exam. Do not date a notice.
- In a memo, key in the *Our ref* as dictated. Do not add your own initials or insert a *Your ref*.
- Key in the text, making amendments as dictated.
- Key in the heading following the capitalisation and underlining instructions.
- Follow capitalisation as dictated for text in the body of the document.
- This document is designed to fit on to an A4 sheet. Single-page documents should not be numbered, but if your letter extends to a second page then the continuation sheet must be numbered. **Insert ➤ Page Numbers** will allow you to customise your numbering.
- Use the **Spellcheck** and proofread the hard copy carefully, particularly checking you have not omitted or misplaced text.

Document 3: report/article

- Key in the text, making amendments according to the draft as you work.
- Key in the heading using the capitalisation as dictated.
- Follow capitalisation as dictated for text in the body of the document.
- When emphasising a sentence or paragraph you may embolden, capitalise,

underline, alter the font style/size, centre or inset. Remember to take the emphasis instruction off at the end of the portion of text.

- When altering the linespacing of paragraphs of text do not forget to change back at the end of the section.
- This document is designed to fit on to an A4 sheet. Single-page documents should not be numbered, but if your letter extends to a second page then the continuation sheet must be numbered. **Insert ➤ Page Numbers** will allow you to customise your numbering.
- Use the **Spellcheck** and proofread carefully, particularly checking you have not omitted or misplaced text.

Accessing audio practice exams material

Candidate Information Sheets

Candidate Information Sheets follow for these practice exams:

- AT 1.A1, AT 1.A2 and AT 1.A3
- AT 1.B1, AT 1.B2 and AT 1.B3
- AT 1.C1, AT 1.C2 and AT 1.C3

Templates

The letter and memo templates are available on the Hodder Plus website at **www.hodderplus.co.uk/ocrtextprocessing**. The same templates can be used for each practice exam.

Dictated documents

The dictation for the above exams is also available on the Hodder Plus website.

EXAM AT 1.A1

CANDIDATE INFORMATION SHEET

Included in dictation:

Gerwyn Rees
Millie Ashleigh
Consumer Help Service

Addresses:

22 Forest Avenue
Burton Joyce
NOTTINGHAM
NG14 7CR

Reference(s):

MA/WTP

NB: All other instructions (eg courtesy titles, headings, etc) will be given in the dictation.

EXAM AT 1.A2

CANDIDATE INFORMATION SHEET

Included in dictation:

Takashi Kondo
Building Inspector
Lloyd Evans
Surveyor and Valuator
5 Albany Crescent Bournemouth

Addresses:

Reference(s):

LE/TK

NB: All other instructions (eg courtesy titles, headings, etc) will be given in the dictation.

EXAM AT 1.A3

CANDIDATE INFORMATION SHEET

Included in dictation:

Arena Leisure Centre
PAT
Fire Safety Log Book

Addresses:

Reference(s):

NB: All other instructions (eg courtesy titles, headings, etc) will be given in the dictation.

EXAM AT 1.B1

CANDIDATE INFORMATION SHEET

Included in dictation:

John Flanagan
English Rose
Gibraltar
Carol Domanski
General Manager

References:

CD/LA

Address:

29 The Meadows
DONCASTER
DN1 7DW

NB: All other instructions (eg courtesy titles, department names, headings etc) will
        be given in the dictation.

EXAM AT 1.B2

CANDIDATE INFORMATION SHEET

Included in dictation:

Gwyn Evans
Eileen Yeo

References:

EY/RH

Address:

NB: All other instructions (eg courtesy titles, department names, headings etc) will
        be given in the dictation.

EXAM AT 1.B3

CANDIDATE INFORMATION SHEET

Included in dictation:

/

References:

/

Address:

/

NB: All other instructions (eg courtesy titles, department names, headings etc) will
       be given in the dictation.

EXAM AT 1.C1

CANDIDATE INFORMATION SHEET

Included in dictation:

Sharon Wood
Donald Redfern
Director of Savings

References:

DR/WK

Address:

168 Hellesdon Drive
LITTLE PLUMSTEAD
Norfolk
NR13 4LT

NB: All other instructions (eg courtesy titles, department names, headings etc) will be given in the dictation.

EXAM AT 1.C2

CANDIDATE INFORMATION SHEET

Included in dictation:

Smith and Brown Insurance
Church Street

References:

Address:

NB: All other instructions (eg courtesy titles, department names, headings etc) will be
given in the dictation.

EXAM AT 1.C3

CANDIDATE INFORMATION SHEET

Included in dictation:

Faster Payments

References:

Address:

NB: All other instructions (eg courtesy titles, department names, headings etc) will be given in the dictation.

5 WORKED EXAMPLES

This section provides worked examples of each practice exercise and exam in this book.

The worked examples show one way of displaying the material, but this will not be the only acceptable way. For example, you may have decided to use different emphasis, your line ends may differ slightly or you may have left extra linespacing after headings. This is acceptable as long as you have followed instructions and formatted your document consistently.

To get the most from this material, carry out each practice exercise or complete exam, then proofread it before referring to this section to check your work.

The workings of each set of exercises and exams for each different unit are grouped together, as follows:

- Text Production practice exercises – TP 1.1 to TP 1.15
- Text Production practice exams – TP 1.A, TP 1.B, TP 1.C
- Word Processing practice exercises – WP 1.1 to WP 1.12
- Word Processing practice exams – WP 1.A, WP 1.B, WP 1.C
- Audio-Transcription practice exercises – AT 1.1 to AT 1.12
- Audio-Transcription practice exams – AT 1.A, AT 1.B, AT 1.C

EXERCISE TP 1.1: WORKED EXAMPLE

Progress Group
Westwood Way
Coventry
CV4 8JQ

024 7647 0033

Our ref CD/WF

30 May 2009

Miss N Burnton
17 Wessex Park Road
BRISTOL
BS3 4NR

Dear Miss Burnton

We are writing to all our shareholders to give details about a proposed company merger. We have pleasure in enclosing an information pack. This will provide answers to many of your questions.

In order for this merger to proceed it is necessary to have the support of our shareholders. A vote will take place at the next monthly meeting. This meeting will be at our head office in Bath city centre. We will write to you as soon as possible to let you know the date and time of the meeting.

You will be able to vote by post or you may attend the meeting in person. Your chairman recommends that you vote in favour of the merger.

We firmly believe that this merger is in the best interests of our company. The merger will allow us to expand our business into many other countries. As a direct result of the merger your company will become financially secure.

We urge you to take the time to read the information pack. Please use your vote wisely.

Yours sincerely

Carol Dunne
Company Secretary

Enc

Progress Group
180 Leopold Road
MULBARTON
Norfolk
NR14 9HZ

01508 777656

Our ref   MM/BC

3 March 2010

Mrs C Richmond
52 Brandon Crescent
TAVERHAM
Norfolk
NR8 2LK

Dear Carolyn

For some time now I have thought that a monthly newsletter would be a good way of passing on information to our volunteers. Enclosed is a copy of the first issue. I hope you will find it helpful. As you will see, details are included of the many training courses open to volunteers.

The next course on fire safety will take place on the first Thursday of next month. This course is mandatory. If you cannot attend on that day, there will be other dates later in the year when you can enrol for this worthwhile training.

I should be grateful if you would complete the tear-off slip at the foot of the newsletter. This is to ensure that your correct details are on file. A contact number in case of an emergency is also required. Please leave your signed form in my pigeon hole when you are next on duty.

I should like to take this opportunity to say how much we appreciate the time and effort given by our volunteers week in week out.

Yours sincerely

Michelle Martin
Volunteer Co-ordinator

Enc

EXERCISE TP 1.3: WORKED EXAMPLE

PROGRESS STORAGE
Freemantle House
48-52 Station Road
BRISTOL
BS2 7KL

Our ref HM/246

3 March 2010

Ms Jayne Fielding
46 Sycamore Street
LEICESTER
LE9 4TP

Dear Ms Fielding

Thank you for your recent enquiry about our storage units. I note that you will soon be leaving college to spend some time travelling and need a safe place to leave your belongings.

We have a new storage facility in Park Place. This is very close to your current address. You can rent a small unit for as little as £6 per week. The cost includes insurance and VAT. The units may be rented for an indefinite period if you pay by direct debit. We would recommend this method of payment if you plan to be out of the country for a long time.

Our units are open 24 hours a day so you have total freedom of access. Your unique PIN code will allow you to enter the compound at all times of the day and night.

If you would like to visit, please telephone me on 443861. A member of my team will give you a guided tour of the facility and will explain how we operate.

I look forward to hearing from you soon.

Yours sincerely

Harry Middleton
Client Support

PROGRESS GROUP

THE RUBY RESTAURANT

BREAKFAST CONFERENCE MENU

The restaurant is conveniently situated on the ground floor of the hotel.

THE BUFFET

Help yourself to a wide variety of items from the buffet.

Cereals with hot or cold milk
Toast and marmalade
Cold meats and cheeses
Fresh fruit salads with yoghurt

COOKED BREAKFASTS

Order hot food from the waiter.

Traditional cooked breakfast including tomatoes, bacon and eggs.

DRINKS

Tea and coffee will be served at your table by the waiter.

A selection of fruit juice is available from the buffet.

THE WHITE HORSE INN

CHEF'S RECOMMENDATIONS

STARTERS

Celery and stilton soup with croutons
Avocado and prawn cocktail
Smoked haddock mousse garnished with salad

MAIN COURSES

Oven-baked turkey marinated in a spicy apricot sauce
Roast leg of lamb with garlic and rosemary
Hungarian style pork chops
Baked stuffed courgettes (vegetarian)

Our main courses are served with a choice of roast, chipped or mashed potatoes and
fresh seasonal vegetables.

DESSERTS

Pears in ginger wine
Fresh strawberry gateau filled with cream
Dutch apple tart with custard
Cheese and biscuits

Coffee and chocolate mints

PROGRESS CENTRAL

The new dining experience in the middle of Birmingham! Come and join us for lunch and enjoy fabulous food at our splendid waterside location.

Our lunch menu includes

Leek and potato soup
Grilled goat's cheese on roasted peppers
Chicken with tarragon sauce
Lemon sole with grapes
Chocolate truffle cake
Lime and passion fruit mousse

Prices start at £8.50 for two courses. The service charge is included.

For a limited period only, we are offering free coffee and mints with all orders.

Telephone us on 298754 for further details.

HEALTH AND SAFETY

The health and safety of all our staff is very important.

We need to train at least six more first aiders. We only have one person on each floor who has been trained in first aid.

Please let your manager know if you would like to be trained for this important role.

First aiders receive a small increase in salary.

The training course lasts five days.

At the end of the course there is an examination.

The company would like two qualified first aiders on each floor.

EXERCISE TP 1.8: WORKED EXAMPLE

REFUSE COLLECTION

NOTICE TO HOUSEHOLDERS LIVING BETWEEN THE OUTER RING ROAD AND THE CITY BOUNDARY

Please note that there will be a change in your black bin collection day. **Collections will now take place one day later.** This new scheme will start next month.

A calendar showing the new days and times will be sent to you shortly.

Please ensure your bins are placed outside before 7 am on the correct day.

The council regrets any inconvenience that this new arrangement may cause. Please contact them if you have a query.

SALE OF LOST PROPERTY

Progress Trains would like to advertise our forthcoming lost property sales.

These will be held at the East Midlands depot on the first Saturday of each month between 9.30 am and 11.30 am.

All proceeds will go to charity.

Items to be sold include

Umbrellas, hats and scarves
Mobile phones
Paperback books
Glasses, purses and other personal items

All goods have been left on Progress Trains. They have remained unclaimed for at least six months.

Please support us. Visit our website www.progresstrains.com for additional information on the sales.

EXERCISE TP 1.10: WORKED EXAMPLE

PROGRESS GROUP ESTATE AGENTS

We are very pleased to be able to offer for sale by public auction the property known as Upper Farm.

There will be three separate lots for auction.

LOT 1

THE FARMHOUSE

The farmhouse includes five bedrooms and a cellar.

LOT 2

THE OUTBUILDINGS

There are four large wooden barns and a brick building which houses the milking equipment.

LOT 3

THE LAND

There are one hundred acres of pasture which are currently used for grazing cattle.

For further details please contact Progress Group Estate Agents.

SEAWARD HOMES

A select development of 2, 3 and 4 bedroom homes on the North Norfolk coast is nearing completion. **The show house is now open and can be viewed by appointment.**

All homes come complete with fully fitted kitchens and carpets. Buyers will have a wide choice of quality and colour. The master bedroom has en suite facilities.

The sea is only a short walk away and the attractive town of Wells with all its amenities is a few minutes by car.

Further details can be found on www.seaward2.co.uk

IS STORAGE A PROBLEM?

Have you run out of space at home? If so, consider renting a storage unit from our firm.

Progress Storage has been providing our satisfied clients with additional storage for over ten years. We are known for our excellent service.

Our modern units offer

Clean and dry storage
Access to your personal possessions day and night
Very competitive rental charges
Town centre locations

If you would like further details of our services, please telephone 443861. Our helpful staff will be pleased to give you a quote.

EXERCISE TP 1.13: WORKED EXAMPLE

SEARCH FOR NEW OFFICES

I have looked at three buildings in the centre of town. In addition, I have inspected an office close to the old trading estate on the outskirts of town. All of the buildings I have seen have some good and bad points. I did not view an office that met all our needs. I am told by local estate agents that premises of the size we require do not come onto the market very often.

However, I think that the building in the High Street meets most of our needs. We should

proceed by asking all the department heads to a meeting. They should arrange a date for a

site visit early next week. We can then discuss a plan for the available space for each

department.

We will need to make some changes to the layout of the space if we decide to proceed with the purchase of the High Street building. The ground floor is one large space and this needs to be divided into smaller rooms. There is <u>no reception</u> and we would need to make a waiting area.

Most of the fittings in the bathrooms are cracked and need to be replaced. The kitchen units are very old and some of the cupboard doors are broken.

The estate agent told me that there were two other firms interested in buying this building for office use. I recommend that we instruct our surveyor to proceed with the survey as soon as possible.

EXERCISE TP 1.14: WORKED EXAMPLE

PROGRESS LANDSCAPES

TIPS FOR THE AMATEUR

This is the first of a series of articles aimed at helping amateurs to undertake simple jobs

around the house and garden.

PAVING

Most paving is laid on sharp sand or on a bed of mortar. Advice should be sought if the area to be paved is subject to heavy use. It is wise to start laying the slabs against a house or garage wall. Then work outwards towards an edge that is flexible. This will avoid having to cut too many stones. Should cutting be necessary, a disc cutter or chisel is recommended. The choice will depend on the depth of the stone. Our company sells and hires out tools for this purpose.

It is most important to use a spirit level to make sure the slabs are even. They should always slope away from the house and garage to prevent flooding.

DECKING

Careful preparation is needed when laying decking. The cleared site should be marked out using pegs and string lines. Joists and deck posts must be placed underneath the decking. Screws are then fixed to secure the platform. All instructions should be read through very carefully before starting the work.

SAFETY

It is sensible to wear gloves when handling wood to avoid splinters. Put on a mask to

prevent inhaling sawdust and treated timbers. If using power tools, goggles are

<u>essential</u>. These will help to protect the eyes.

Our next article will give tips on how to build a greenhouse.

PROGRESS MONEY

A SAFE INVESTMENT

For your peace of mind during these uncertain times, why not invest your money with us?

Progress Money has a fine reputation for taking care of its clients' money. Do not risk your money with other, less reputable organisations when we can help your savings grow.

One of our most popular products at the moment is our 3-year fixed rate bond. This is designed for long-term investments. It offers an interest rate which is fixed for 3 years. The smallest amount you can invest in this account is £1,000. There is no maximum amount. We are offering an interest rate of 3.75 per cent per annum. At the end of the term, the interest rate will match the Bank of England base rate.

If you take out this product, you should note that you are not allowed to withdraw any money during the first year. After this time you may take out all or part of your investment by cheque. However, you will lose interest on the sum invested.

Interest is worked out on a daily basis and you will receive it once a year. Income tax may be deducted. Some people may be able to reclaim any tax paid. Check with your tax office if you are unsure.

Progress Money has branches across the United Kingdom. For details of your nearest branch, or to request a list of our products, please call Customer Services on 08081 579832. We look forward to hearing from you.

EXAM TP 1.A1: WORKED EXAMPLE

Progress Group
Westwood Way
Coventry
CV4 8JQ

024 7647 0033

Our ref BK/EH

6 June 2009

Mrs J Devon
64 Orchard Crescent
WELLINGTON
Somerset
TA21 1PR

Dear Mrs Devon

Thank you for your recent letter about the post of audio typist. I enclose an application form which you should complete. Please return this to me by Friday next week.

If you are chosen to attend for an interview I will contact you again. The selection process will include an English test and an audio typing test. I need to be sure that your English skills are very good and that you are a fast typist.

The typing section is based in our Taunton office. We need to employ six more typists to work in this office. One of our major clients has asked if we can complete some extra work for them. In order for us to be able to do this work we have to employ more staff.

I look forward to receiving copies of your examination certificates and your application form. Please contact me if you have any questions.

If you do not hear from me within the next two weeks you may assume that your application has not been a success.

Yours sincerely

Bethany Kane
Production Manager

Enc

PROGRESS SHOE SHOP

Please note that we are moving to a larger shop very soon.

The new shop is next door and was, until the end of last year, a bank.

After we move we will have sufficient space for a new department.

We will be able to stock a wide range of walking and climbing boots.

Please ask a member of staff if you would like further details about the new shop.

There will be many special discounts during the first week.

We look forward to your continued custom.

SAVING AND INVESTMENTS WITH PROGRESS BANK

There are many reasons why you should open a savings account with this bank. We offer our customers a wide range of investment opportunities. You may want your money to be safe or you may be happy to take some small risks. We can provide you with either type of saving plan.

Our experienced staff will be pleased to discuss our saving plans with you. Perhaps

you would like a savings account with easy access or you may be happy to invest your

money for three years or more. Whatever your needs are we have a savings plan that

will suit you.

Opening an account is very easy when you bank with Progress. There is a simple form to complete before we can process your application. This form can be completed in your local branch or on our web site. New customers can only open an account by going to their local branch. We will need to check your identity if you do not currently bank with us. We have a <u>legal duty</u> to confirm who you are and where you live. This applies to each person when accounts are opened in joint names. New customers also need to provide two samples of their signature. We keep all these signatures. They are referred to by bank staff when money is withdrawn from the bank.

If you would like an appointment to discuss your savings please telephone us or call into your local branch.

PROGRESS PARTY FOODS
16 Grange Park Road
WELWYN GARDEN CITY
AL7 9TC

01632 960032

Our Ref MF/36

3 March 2010

Mrs Julia McDade
14 Windsor Avenue
STEVENAGE
SG7 4XP

Dear Mrs McDade

Thank you for calling at the office last week. It was very helpful to be able to discuss your exact requirements in greater detail. Please confirm that you plan to invite 30 guests to your husband's birthday lunch.

I have had an opportunity to prepare a quotation. I hope you will find it acceptable. The cost of our luxury buffet for 30 people will be £450 plus VAT. A ten per cent deposit will be required.

Our luxury buffet option comprises four separate meat and fish platters plus a selection of quiches and salads. These are followed by small dishes of strawberries and cream along with a range of other desserts and fresh fruit.

All the items are attractively presented on silver serving dishes. The sizing of the portions ensures that guests can remain standing whilst they enjoy their lunch.

Soft drinks and juices are included in the price. Wines are available at extra cost.

I enclose a copy of our brochure which gives detailed information about our buffets. I look forward to hearing from you.

Yours sincerely

Martina Felton
Managing Director

Enc

CHILDREN'S PARTIES

Progress Party Foods can supply a wide variety of food for any occasion. Parties, in particular, are our speciality.

We are always happy to discuss your personal menu choices.

This month we launch a new children's party line.

The delicious menu includes

Pirate ship platter
Savoury bites
Fruit salad selection
Organic gingerbread men
Chocolate pirate ship cake

Each menu is sufficient to feed twelve hungry children. The cost is £5 per head plus delivery. We also supply healthy lunch boxes for children on the move.

Call us now!

EXAM TP 1.B3: WORKED EXAMPLE

PROGRESS PARTY FOODS

A TASTE OF EXCELLENCE

Whatever the occasion, Progress Party Foods can provide you with perfect food choices to suit all your guests. Our company has been in the catering business for fifteen years and we have earned a reputation for quality and style.

Our menus are designed for all age groups. We cater for children's parties, wedding breakfasts and retirement lunches. We can cook for a dinner party if you wish. In all cases we aim to provide a balance of healthy foods and gourmet delights. We will always suggest healthy options. Let us know if you or your guests have special dietary needs.

Our ingredients are sourced locally. Local farmers supply us with top quality produce. Most of our menus reflect seasonal changes. We like to serve food which is at its best.

Our brochure lists our buffet options. You can choose from several themed menus. In all cases, soft drinks and juices are included in the price. Wine can be ordered at additional cost. Alternatively, you may wish to use your own supplier. The choice is yours.

Children's parties are very popular. We offer various options, including lunch boxes for children whose birthday treat involves an excursion with friends. You will be surprised how economical these can be. Prices start at £5 per person plus delivery.

Why not invite us to cater for your next event? We are offering new customers a ten per cent discount. Ring 253761 and request our latest brochure.

EXAM TP 1.C1: WORKED EXAMPLE

Progress Group
Westwood Way
COVENTRY
CV4 8JQ

024 7647 0033

Our Ref   PW/AY

3 March 2010

Mr C Lynch
28 Chapel Square
WALCOTT
Norfolk
NR12 9VX

Dear Mr Lynch

We are pleased to learn that you have chosen to renew your car insurance with us once again. Your new policy is enclosed.

We can also provide cover for your home, life and even your pet. Our home insurance includes all buildings. This takes in sheds and items left in the garden overnight. Buying life cover means that your family would be looked after should you die within the term of your contract. If you have a cat or dog, then our pet insurance will save you having to pay out large sums of money for veterinary fees. Older pets are covered too.

In addition, our company can help you manage your finances. This applies to savings and credit card payments. Our direct saver account is easy to open with as little as £1. Fixed loans are also available. The amount offered will depend on your credit rating. The sum borrowed can be repaid over a set period of time to suit you.

To find out more, please contact the number given on this letterhead.

Yours sincerely

Philip Wainwright
Insurance Adviser

Enc

EXAM TP 1.C2: WORKED EXAMPLE

PROGRESS GROUP

SALES EXECUTIVE

We are looking for an experienced and highly motivated person to lead our sales team based in Norfolk.

Good communication skills are required. You must also be able to build up first-class client relations. To succeed in this post you will show a strong desire to achieve our sales targets. **Working as a team member is vital.**

Please apply in writing within the next 2 weeks with a curriculum vitae to Progress Group, Progress House, Westwood Way, Coventry, CV4 8JQ. Interviews will be held early next month.

PROGRESS GROUP HOLDS ITS GROUND

BRIEF REPORT TO SHAREHOLDERS

In spite of a troubled year worldwide, the Progress Group has continued to hold its ground. Activities in sales, building and marketing all show pleasing results. The organisation is therefore able to carry on the upward trend of recent years. Group turnover increased by a modest 5% and net sales were also up compared to last year.

All our past hard work has helped us to create a <u>solid base</u>. Our business model has proved itself. However, we cannot rest on our laurels. Challenges are always present both inside and outside the group. New systems and processes have to be tested and we must move with the times. Long term social and economic trends must also be taken into account.

One of our main goals at present is to expand our customer base. Marketing campaigns are helping to achieve this. This year, for instance, the sales of our own brand of products have been greatly enhanced by putting large sums of money into advertising.

We are still active in looking after our buildings. In this respect those outlets not reaching their targets are being sold off. The income received will be invested in those where potential growth has been forecast.

With the above in mind, the group looks set to achieve good results in all aspects of its business in the years to come.

We look forward to seeing many of our members at the Annual General Meeting next month.

EXAM WP 1.1: WORKED EXAMPLE

END OF TERM REPORT

Most of the students on the legal audio typing course have worked hard this term and have reached the required standards.

The department head and the class teacher held meetings with each student during the final week of term. Progress to date was discussed as well as any concerns the student had about their course work.

Some members of the class said that they would like more English lessons. It has

therefore been decided to begin classes on a Tuesday morning at 9.30am instead of

10.30am. This hour will be an English lesson. The early start on Tuesdays will take

effect from the first week of next term.

The programme for weekly tests was distributed. Details of the pass marks and the final examination at the end of next term were given to the students.

> Kay Potter was ill last term. Although she was sent work to do at home she has been unable to keep up with the rest of the group. Therefore it has been decided that she should withdraw from this course and join the next course which is due to commence in September. We understand from her parents that she is making a good recovery. Most members of the class have sent her cards.

The need to complete homework on time was stressed. There are two class members who are falling behind the rest of the group. These two were given extra homework to complete during the holiday.

All the students are very happy and eager to complete their final term so that they can start on their chosen careers.

270

C:\REPORT.doc

MINIMISING RISK

Daily life can be dangerous. Many of the actions we take have an associated risk. Some people are happy to accept that risk. Others prefer to take out insurance to cover themselves against accidents and hazards.

At Progress Insurance we have a range of policies to cover most of life's dangers. Premiums are low and can be reduced further by accepting an excess which is payable on any claims made.

One of the most important insurances that householders can take out is house

and contents cover. This insures the policyholder against damage to a dwelling

and its contents. Should the property be burgled or damaged, a claim can be

made to replace the items affected. Many people underestimate the value of

their furnishings, so it is very important to review the figure on a regular basis.

Car drivers will understand the importance of motor insurance. Comprehensive insurance covers the driver and any car driven. Third party insurance covers the policyholder only against damage caused to the other person and vehicle. People who drive inexpensive vehicles often opt for this policy because the annual charge is much cheaper.

Travel insurance is another safeguard that is offered to the general public. Single trip or annual cover will protect the traveller against delays, cancellations and loss of luggage or money. Although this insurance is a sensible precaution, many people think it is too expensive and are willing to take the risk when travelling.

If you would like a personalised quotation on any of our policies, contact Progress Insurance now on 024 7647 0033. We look forward to receiving your call.

267

C:\INSURE.doc

EXERCISE WP 1.3: WORKED EXAMPLE

INDUCTION PROCEDURE

A new induction procedure is being drawn up. The responsibility for delivering the majority of the induction is being transferred to departments. Human Resources will still have overall responsibility and will provide guidelines.

The aim is to give information in several ways and not to overload the new recruit with too much information. Interactive programs are being used. These have the advantage that the new employee can go through them several times at a steady pace.

There will be a central induction of a full day, which will take place every 6 weeks, to which all new employees will be invited.

Information from Personnel will now be done online with an interactive program and includes several online quizzes.

The building tour should not be restricted to just where the new employee will be working. It is suggested that this is done during the first day. It should provide a useful guide to the whole building.

The health and safety briefing will be done with an interactive program. This will give a

good overview of the important points. Line managers must go through specific points

relating to the recruit's job.

> Line managers must ensure that the new employee understands the job role and how it links in to the business as a whole. We are introducing a "buddy" system. Line managers will need to allocate a colleague, who is not the line manager, to mentor the recruit. The aim is to provide a point of contact for any routine queries.

Please let us have any ideas to improve the procedure.

261

C:\INDUCTION2.doc

EXERCISE WP 1.4: WORKED EXAMPLE

SECRETARIAL AND BUSINESS STUDIES COURSES

At the end of last term the building was modernised.

The canteen has been refitted and new tables and chairs have been purchased.

All classrooms have <u>new computers and printers</u>.

Enrol by the end of this month for the following courses:

Getting the best from your computer
Medical typing
Word processing
Touch typing
Speed keying
Legal typing

Course teachers will be happy to talk with prospective students in order to offer advice.

There will be teachers available on Monday and Tuesday mornings until the end of the month.

There is no need to make an appointment.

For a guided tour of the new building please ask at the main reception.

EXERCISE WP 1.5: WORKED EXAMPLE

PHOTOGRAPHY COURSES AT PROGRESS COLLEGE

Do you like to take photographs? Are you disappointed with the results? Would you like to learn new techniques?

If the answer to any of the above questions is yes, why not consider enrolling on a photography course at Progress College? Next term we have a wide range of courses on offer.

Learn how to photograph

people
pets
plants
places

under expert tuition

Our spacious photographic studios offer first-class facilities. Courses are held during the day and in the evening. <u>We even run a Saturday class</u>.

Come along to our Open Day next month. Our tutors will be there to answer your questions.

EXERCISE WP 1.6: WORKED EXAMPLE

OFFICE EQUIPMENT EXHIBITION

There will be an exhibition of a range of equipment suitable for the small office.

Come along to see the latest equipment.

Next Wednesday in the Town Hall Chambers from 10.00 am to 8.00 pm.

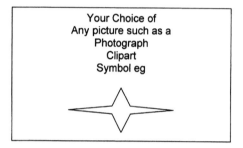

Over 20 exhibitors have taken stands and there will be demonstrations running throughout the day. It is a good opportunity to ask questions.

Stands include

Colour printers
Small, easy to use photocopiers
Desks and chairs
Laptops and notebooks
Binders and laminators
Telephones

There are also stands giving good prices on a wide range of stationery and other items.

<u>Have a free cup of coffee</u> with this advertisement.

EXERCISE WP 1.7: WORKED EXAMPLE

FIRE MARSHALS

The safety of all employees is of paramount importance. For this reason we will undertake a practice evacuation of the building one day next week. Each department has its own fire marshal who will be responsible for all staff leaving the building in an orderly manner.

Employees are requested to familiarise themselves with the fire escape routes, evacuation procedures and assembly points. In order to ensure that everyone is out of the building each floor has been given a unique assembly point which is in the courtyard outside the main entrance.

Names and extension numbers of all the departmental fire marshals are given below.

FIRE MARSHAL	DEPARTMENT	EXTENSION
Andrew Newcombe	General office	908
Paula Tang	Marketing and sales	145
Lucy Cole	Payroll and accounts	768
Anne Gibson	Photocopying	954
Daniel Collins	Advertising	723
Victoria Jones	Warehouse and stock	879
Meena Poole	Publishing	409
Brenda Patel	Personnel	378
Diane Hopwood	Reception	975
Karen Wong	Services	287
Mary Gilbert	Canteen and catering	705
Julie Perry	Training and development	412
Colin Hogan	Quality control	531
James Laws	Stationery and supplies	691

PROGRESS STATIONERY SUPPLIES

All our products can be purchased via our website. Alternatively our Customer Service Team will be happy to take your order. We aim to deliver within 4 working days.

Send us a copy of your logo and we can print it on any of our products. In this way you can coordinate your stationery for a truly professional look. When placing your order, please ensure that you indicate clearly the colour and quantity required.

Contact us now to see how you can benefit from a 20% discount on your first order.

Here is a list of our most popular lines this month.

ITEM	DESCRIPTION	PACK SIZE
Business cards	Premium business cards in silver case	250
Letterhead	A4 letterhead on 90 gsm paper	100
Envelopes	DL envelopes to match letterhead	50
Return address labels	Sticky labels incorporating logo	150
Folded notecards	Personalised notecards with logo	50
Postcards	A6 blank cards	100
Compliments slips	Printed with your details	100
Rubber stamp	Self inking stamp with logo	1
Tee shirt	Cotton tee shirt with logo on pocket	1

EXERCISE WP 1.9: WORKED EXAMPLE

CAR PERMIT NUMBER CHANGES

Some staff are being given a new car permit number. This is to incorporate the members of staff coming from the Newhall office. The members of staff listed have new numbers. New discs need to be collected from Michelle Dyer in the General Office. Her extension number is 3498.

All members of staff must display their car permit disc on their windscreen. Failure to do this may result in the use of the permit being taken away.

NAME	JOB TITLE	CAR PERMIT
Allen Greta	Creche Supervisor	267
Andrew Harris	Communications Officer	222
Boothe Sharon	Cash Office Assistant	398
Connelly Kevin	Training Co-ordinator	220
Desforges Jen	Help Desk Supervisor	342
Fernandez Marco	Sales Assistant	268
Flint Mavis	Nursery Worker	267
Heath Sara Jane	Marketing Sales Manager	290
Hill Bill	Building Services Officer	351
Jones Katie Anne	Payroll Officer	397
Khan Zafar	Help Desk Assistant	340
Maseuleo Annette	Sales Assistant Manager	265
Oder Peter	Purchase Manager	292
Patel Maz	Telephone Sales Manager	334
Potter Anna Maria	Canteen Manager	321
Wilkinson John	Chief Receptionist	341
Williams Sian	Information Assistant	285

EXERCISE WP 1.10: WORKED EXAMPLE

RETURNED GOODS FORM

FULL NAME OF CUSTOMER	Mrs Jane Wilson
HOME ADDRESS	71 Old Oak Road Belvedere Kent DA17 1NR
DAYTIME TELEPHONE NUMBER	020 7461 4063
EVENING TELEPHONE NUMBER	020 7461 4064
ORDER NUMBER	2160
REASON FOR RETURN	Arrived too late for the birthday party

CODE	DEPARTMENT	DESCRIPTION
50A	Paper goods	Red disposable drinking cups
30B	Decorations	Balloons and paper chains
10C	Paper goods	Blue floral patterned plates
40E	Household linens	Square plastic table cloths
20F	Paper goods	Red and blue napkins
10H	Decorations	Silk flowers for table centres

Please arrange for a ~~replacement~~/refund* for the customer

DATE	14 June 2009

* Delete as appropriate using strikethrough

EXERCISE WP 1.11: WORKED EXAMPLE

GROUP BOOKING FORM

PROVIDER	Progress Cookery School
VENUE	Redruth House Longtown Road Banbury OX4 8TV
TELEPHONE NUMBER	01632 960537
GROUP LEADER	Ms Gemma Wilkinson
ADDRESS	46 Mountsorrel Road Leamington Spa CV31 2GX
CONTACT NUMBER	07776 387662
EMAIL ADDRESS	gemmaw@quickchat.co.uk
NAMES OF GROUP MEMBERS	Miss Maddie Turner Mrs Judy Greville Mrs Sally de Souza Ms Hanna Blake Mrs Tina Doyle

COURSES BOOKED

COURSE	LEVEL	COST
Sharpen Those Knife Skills	Elementary	£140
Italian Desserts and Biscuits	Intermediate	£165
A Perfect Summer Supper Party	Intermediate	£200
Passionate about Patisserie	Advanced	£220

Group Leader is entitled/~~not entitled~~* to one free place

DATE	Day Month Year

* Delete as appropriate using strikethrough

EXERCISE WP 1.12: WORKED EXAMPLE

COURSE APPLICATION FORM

NAME	Joe Wood	
JOB ROLE	Assistant Sales Manager	
HOME ADDRESS	Flat 2 34 Trent Lane HARROGATE HG1 5TP	
TELEPHONE NUMBER	0163 296 0457	
FAX NUMBER	0163 296 4680	
TITLE OF COURSE	LOCATION	LENGTH (NUMBER OF DAYS, WEEKS)
Introduction to Presentation Skills	Wakefield	2 days
Client Care (Part 1)	Leeds	3 days
Child Protection	Head Office	1 day
Induction to the Company	Head Office	1 day
Telephone Skills	Manchester	2 days
Advanced Selling Methods	Training Centre	18 weeks
Team Building (Part 2)	Chester	1 week

Manager's approval has/~~has not~~ been given.*

DATE	Date of Task

* Delete as appropriate using strikethrough

MACHINE SHORTHAND

Machines have been used to record the spoken word for many years. The very first machine was made in 1830 and only recorded symbols on a paper tape. There have been many changes to the machine since then. Today the symbols are saved to an internal memory.

> After the shorthand writer has taken down the spoken word the symbols are then moved to a computer. Then the computer translates this information into text. Until about thirty years ago the symbols would have been read and then typed from the paper tape.

There are a number of training courses. Trainee shorthand writers must have a good knowledge of grammar in order to prepare their documents. Some courses include lessons on the English language.

Trainees will be writing at a speed of 180 words per minute at the end of their course. This speed will be adequate to deal with most types of work. Some very skilled people have passed tests at 300 words per minute.

This is a very skilled career. There are job opportunities with companies specialising in

the supply of transcripts. These companies provide transcripts of court hearings,

interviews, tribunals and meetings. The work can be completed very quickly because a

computer converts the shorthand into text.

The hours of work vary depending on the type of job and there is not a daily routine. This is an exciting and very rewarding career.

People working in this field travel all over the country and overseas doing a range of work. They meet many interesting people and visit new places during the course of their careers.

268

C:\SHORTHAND.doc

EXHIBITION OF KITCHEN EQUIPMENT

Town Hall
25 High Street
Chippenham
Wiltshire
SN14 3LT

Telephone 01249 445611

We will have well-known chefs giving demonstrations.

As well as kitchen gadgets and equipment there will be a wide range of speciality foods for visitors to purchase. Most stands will have <u>free samples to give away</u>.

The following is a list of some of the items being demonstrated.

Food processors and hand blenders
Ice cream and yoghurt makers
Pressure cookers and steamers
Ceramic storage containers

The cafe will be open all day and will serve hot and cold refreshments.

Tickets cost £8 per person on the door, but if you order your tickets in advance you will save £2.

PROGRESS HOLIDAY SITES

Our holiday sites have excellent facilities and are situated in prime locations. Each site has a general store selling toiletries and groceries, a heated swimming pool and entertainment is provided in the clubhouse during the evenings.

There are many types of accommodation available for visitors. We have a wide range of properties with four bedrooms suitable for large families. There are also smaller properties with one bedroom for couples. All accommodation has a well-equipped kitchen, bath or shower and a television.

We have some sites in seaside locations as well as some situated in woodland giving lovely views over surrounding countryside.

Types of property are listed below.

PROPERTY	LOCATION	SITE
Detached chalets	Devon	10
Mobile homes	Cornwall	12
Thatched cottages	Dorset	14
Studio flats and apartments	Somerset	16
Hostel accommodation	Avon	18
Detached houses	Shropshire	20
Tents and caravans	North Yorkshire	22
Terraced chalets	Norfolk	24
Detached bungalows	Kent	26
Narrow boats and barges	West Sussex	28
Bed and breakfast	Essex	30
Penthouse flats	Hampshire	32
Converted barns	Wiltshire	34
Villas and wooden lodges	East Sussex	36

EXAM WP 1.A4: WORKED EXAMPLE

CUSTOMER ORDER FORM

COMPANY NAME	Progress Group International
COMPANY ADDRESS	Progress House Westwood Way Coventry CV4 8JQ
CONTACT NAME	Mrs Rebecca Watson
TITLE	General Office Manager
TELEPHONE NUMBER	024 7647 0033
FAX NUMBER	024 7646 8080
ACCOUNT NUMBER	4678
DELIVERY INSTRUCTIONS	By overnight courier

QUANTITY	COLOUR	ITEM
10	Black	Bound A4 note books
50 reams	White	A4 copy paper
10 boxes	Brown	Heavy duty envelopes
10	Navy blue	Standard box files
20 packets	Gold	Giant staples
10 boxes	Assorted	Coloured pencils
10	Royal blue	A4 desk diaries

These items are/~~are not~~* required urgently

DATE	8 June 2009

* Delete as appropriate using strikethrough

EXAM WP 1.B1: WORKED EXAMPLE

RECYCLING STRATEGY

In line with Government targets to reduce the amount of waste sent to landfill, Westholme District Council is making recycling as simple as possible for its residents.

This year we have managed to reduce the amount of waste sent to landfill by almost 32%, a figure which compares very favourably with other councils in the United Kingdom.

So, what exactly do we do to encourage you to recycle? Every household is provided with a black wheelie bin, a green bin and a red recycling box. All three containers are collected on a weekly basis. All you have to do is position them at the edge of your property by 0800 on the specified day.

> Your recycling box can contain papers, magazines and bottles (glass and plastic). All other household waste should be placed in your black bin. Food and garden waste should be put in the green bin. The contents of this bin will be composted, so it is vital that you do not include other types of waste.

If you live in a flat you may not have access to individual recycling bins, but there will be communal bins for your building.

Elderly or disabled people who cannot handle their bins can request an assisted

collection. The Council will collect the household waste from their door.

Every household is also entitled to one free collection of three items of bulky material every three months. Bulky material includes items such as fridges, cookers and furniture. Please ensure that you give the Council ten days' notice when you book your collection date.

263

C:\STRATEGY.doc

BEACH HUTS FOR HIRE

The redevelopment of the South Promenade is now complete. We have opened a new children's playground next to the Pier. In addition, a beach bar and café have started trading.

We have constructed 50 beach huts. These are located on Westholme Chine. They are available for hire, with immediate effect.

Rental charges start at £15 per day.

Daily rental begins at 0800 and ends at 2000.

Our beach huts offer

uninterrupted views of the bay
a café within walking distance
piped drinking water nearby
free local parking

Why not hire a hut this summer? **Give us a call on 01632 960529.** We look forward to hearing from you.

EXAM WP 1.B3: WORKED EXAMPLE

HIGHWAYS DEPARTMENT – SCHEDULE OF WORK

Within the next few weeks, Westholme District Council staff will be undertaking a number of key projects on roads around the district. Notice is hereby given to the public that the work listed below will commence shortly.

It is likely that temporary traffic lights will have to be installed at some locations to minimise traffic congestion. We will notify local residents in advance of any major disruption. We will also keep our website updated. Please avoid these areas wherever possible.

We apologise for any inconvenience caused by this essential work. Please contact us on 01632 960527 for further information.

LOCATION	WORK TO BE UNDERTAKEN	DURATION (DAYS)
Amberley Road	Re-surface road and pavements	8
Brierley Gardens	Install cycle track	5
Clumber Terrace	Install pelican crossing	4
Finedon Place	Replace traffic lights	5
Harold Street	Upgrade street lighting	2
Kingston Avenue	Install chicanes along route	8
Matthew Court	Install additional street lights	3
Newton Drive	Lop and remove overhanging branches	2
Parkhurst Square	Remove bollards and no entry signs	3
Selby Road	Paint double yellow lines	1

EXAM WP 1.B4: WORKED EXAMPLE

MOBILITY ASSESSMENT FORM

NAME OF APPLICANT	Mr Geoffrey William Atkins
ADDRESS	41 Ashley Road Coombe Park Westleigh BN42 5JL
TELEPHONE	01632 960852
DATE OF BIRTH	14 November 1928
NATURE OF DISABILITY	Severe arthritis in joints Difficulty in walking Inability to climb stairs
NAME OF ASSESSOR	Jeanette McVitie
CONTACT NUMBERS	Office: 01632 960524 extension 2017 Mobile: 07776 997308

ACTIONS REQUIRED

CODE	DESCRIPTION	TIMING
3298	External handrails to front and back doors	Immediate
3241	Indoor walking frame	Immediate
5376	Shower chair	Immediate
6871	Intercom system linked to Councilcare	Within a month

Applicant will require/~~not require~~* daily help

DATE	Day Month Year

* Delete as appropriate using strikethrough

LAMINATOR

I have been asked to include, in this newsletter, some tips on how to use the laminator.

An A4 laminator has been bought for the office. It will laminate paper and photographs so will be ideal for laminating notices.

A supply of A4, (a packet of 50), and A3, (a packet of 25), pouches has been purchased. A5 and smaller pouches can be bought. Please be careful not to waste pouches as they are very expensive.

The pouches are water resistant and can be wiped clean.

Staff are very welcome to use the laminator for private use if they buy their own pouches which are available from Kelly Harding.

Switch off and unplug the laminator when not in use. Do not use the laminator close to water or spill water on the laminator, the cord or wall socket. Only use the laminator for paper and photographs. This laminator will not do thicker items.

Ensure that the laminator is where there is plenty of space for the pouch to go

through easily. Turn the machine on and wait for a green light.

Do a test run before doing anything which is important such as a one-off photograph.

> Always put the item in a pouch. Never laminate an empty pouch. Place the item inside the pouch against the sealed edge. Place pouch, sealed edge first, into the laminator slot. Keep the pouch straight and use the edge guide to centre it.

Immediately remove the laminated item from the back of the machine. Let the item cool on a flat surface for several seconds before turning it off.

266

C:\LAMINATOR2.doc

EXAM WP 1.C2: WORKED EXAMPLE

TECHNICAL BRIEFINGS

It has been agreed that there is a need for regular technical briefings. This is in response to several requests from staff who think that email briefings are not working.

Information will still be sent by email to all staff.

The meetings will concentrate on any points where demonstrations are useful.

<u>All staff must attend</u> these monthly meetings to keep up to date.

Your Choice of
Any picture such as a
Photograph
Clipart
Symbol eg

We are hoping to recruit two members of staff to deliver these staff briefings. Training and support will be given. **If you are interested please contact Jon Mould on extension 3245.** Applicants will be expected to give a short presentation at the interview.

EXAM WP 1.C3: WORKED EXAMPLE

LOCAL AGENTS

The number of clients assigned to each agent varies from month to month. These figures were taken at the beginning of last month. Three agents have only been working for us for 6 months. Their client numbers are low. It takes, on average, a year to build up client numbers.

It is hoped that with increased sales all agents will have a minimum number of 500 clients. At the present time there is no need to recruit any more agents.

AGENT NAME	ADDRESS	CLIENT NUMBERS
James Harding	Oakdale Square	567
Denise Gumbrill	The Walkway	290
Peggy Smith	New Road	623
Jon Muir	Station Mews	587
Rasool Afzal	Shelley Park Road	555
Margaret Erskine	Broadway Crescent	523
Shahid Iqbal	Elm Street	612
Vanessa Chan	Fir Tree Avenue	573
Maz Mann	Pelier Place	380
June Kohler	Mather Road	590
Kim Betts	Grove Road	602
Sally Ann Devine	Ivory Drive	455
Maureen Willets	Heather Lea Lane	571
Steve Rocca	Main Crescent	633
Bob Singh	Ridings Way	538
Hazel Quinn	Timber Road	570
Pat McEvoy	East Bank Road	505
Matt Taylor	Naylor Place	537

EXAM WP 1.C4: WORKED EXAMPLE

DELIVERY NOTE

TITLE (MR, MRS, MS)	Ms	
FIRST NAME(S)	Anne Marie	
SURNAME	Baker	
HOME ADDRESS	94 Archers Circle Birmingham B15 3EA	
TELEPHONE NUMBER	0121 496 5218	
ALTERNATIVE DELIVERY ADDRESS	103 Archers Circle Birmingham B15 2EZ	
ALTERNATIVE TELEPHONE NUMBER	0121 496 9367	
DESCRIPTION OF ITEM	STOCK CODE	NUMBER
A4 packet of white multiuse 90g paper	P34	10
500 sheets of cream card	C23	3
Gloss A4 laminating pouches	L12	4
Box of white laser labels	LL10	2
Pack of manilla self-seal C5 envelopes	E67	10
Laser A4 multipack of 5 colours	P54	2

New/~~existing~~ customer.*

DATE	Date of Task

* Delete as appropriate using strikethrough

DOCUMENT 1

Rajesh Shashi
Chartered Accountants
Moat House Mews
CHESTER
CH1 8CK
Telephone – 01244 505050

Our ref TK/QK

Miss Aruna Dipak
Swan Cottage
Mill Pond Lane
Mickle Trafford
CHESTER
CH3 7MD

6th June 2009

Dear Miss Dipak

BOUTIQUE ASIANNA

I enclose the accounts for the above business for your consideration.

You have incurred a lot of expense during the year with respect to your interior and exterior redecoration costs. Water rates and insurance remain steady but there has been a very sharp rise in electricity costs. After taking all these expenses into account there is a loss of £4000. This is quite normal for the first year of trading. There is a tax charge of £21 from the bank interest received.

If you are happy with the accounts as they stand please would you sign where shown. They need to be returned to me as soon as possible. Once they have been finalised I will prepare the necessary tax return form.

If you have any queries please do not hesitate to contact me straight away.

Yours sincerely

Tanvir Kabir
Senior Accountant

Enc

EXERCISE AT 1.2: WORKED EXAMPLE

DOCUMENT 1

Progress Group
Westwood Way
COVENTRY
CV4 8JQ

024 7647 0033

3 March 2010

Our ref CB/PT

Mrs Lorraine Finlayson
193 Station Road
COLWYN BAY
LL28 9XT

Dear Mrs Finlayson

MOTOR INSURANCE STANDING ORDER

I am writing to inform you that the payment for your vehicle insurance has not been paid this month. This is because there were insufficient funds in your account. I must stress that you should not exceed your agreed overdraft limit of £500. Otherwise all direct debits and standing orders may not be paid. A separate charge is made for every payment refused. I enclose a list of your current direct debits and standing orders.

In order to stabilise your account I think it would be best to have a meeting. It may help you to know that I work the first Saturday in every month from 9 am to 1 pm. If this time suits you I suggest you contact my secretary, Linda Hardwick, to arrange an appointment.

I look forward to resolving this matter.

Yours faithfully

Colin Bacchus
Manager

Enc

Progress Group
180 Leopold Road
MULBARTON
Norfolk
NR14 9HZ

01508 777656

Our ref   JW/AD

3 March 2010

Mr Trevor Cousins
38 Western Park Avenue
HAPTON
Norfolk
NR31 6WG

Dear Mr Cousins

KITCHEN DESIGN

As you have recently bought some goods from us we are enclosing a trade account form. We hope this may be of help to you in the future.

We thought you should know that we now have a kitchen designer at our showroom. He will be able to help you with your new kitchen design. He will also give you a quotation free of charge. If you have received an estimate from someone else we will promise to match it.

Our company not only gives advice on kitchens but also on windows and stairs. A representative will visit your home and take measurements. Then he will quote you a very good price.

Please contact us for details of the special discount weeks that we hold from time to time. We look forward to hearing from you.

Yours sincerely

Julia Webb
Customer Service Manager

Enc

EXERCISE AT 1.4: WORKED EXAMPLE

DOCUMENT 2

MEMORANDUM

TO: Ciaran Doherty, Customer Liaison Department

FROM: Marcus Osbert, Service Manager

REF: MO/WP

DATE: today

Recall Notification for Prowess Astute

The Prowess Astute quality control programme has found a fault with the automatic gearbox on the Lady Vixen model.

In order to correct this problem it will be necessary to replace the automatic gearbox and the cooling fan. The work will be carried out free of charge to all current owners.

My secretary will be writing to those owners concerned during the next two weeks. All owners will be asked to make an appointment with the service department. Please make sure that each person concerned is given high priority.

A special helpline number will be set up for this purpose.

DOCUMENT 2

MEMORANDUM

To   All Parish Councillors

From   Clerk to the Council

Date   Date for today

Ref   MDG/DH

<u>May Day Gala</u>

I am pleased to report that the gala this year broke all previous records. There were more people attending. The number of stalls increased from 24 to 33.

Although the event is not organised as a profit making venture a surplus of £3,000 has been made. This amount includes donations from local businesses.

In the past any surplus money has been used for helping local organisations. Perhaps this year consideration could be given to putting this surplus towards setting up a wildlife section on the village green. Funds could be used to purchase 2 wooden benches to be placed near the playing fields.

MEMORANDUM

To: Jo Daniels

From: Alistair McEvoy

Date: Day Month Year

Ref: AM/DH

Interviews for the post of Junior Secretary

The interview panel for the above post has now agreed on a date. This has been fixed for Thursday of next week.

I should be grateful if you would email the five applicants on the shortlist. They should be informed of their interview times. They will also need to have precise details as to how to find our office block.

I suggest that the first candidate comes at 10 am. We will aim to finish at 4 pm allowing an hour for lunch. Each interview should take about three quarters of an hour.

Please keep the panel informed of these arrangements.

DOCUMENT 2

The Successful Personal Assistant

The role of the PA has developed in recent years. Greater knowledge and responsibility are required. Sable distant learning course has been designed to give a sound understanding of key areas of organisation. It is designed to fit around your current commitments.

Personal development and people skills are features of this course. You will learn how to resolve conflict and improve your negotiation skills. You will then be able to manage your own schedule more efficiently.

The course covers ten modules each lasting around three to four hours. There will be access to help and support at all times.

Please contact your section head for further details and an enrolment form.

DOCUMENT 2

Development Plans

The outline plans for the development of the leisure facilities and outdoor sports areas will be on display in the Parish Rooms. It is proposed to display these plans for four weeks starting the first week in June.

The Parish Clerk will be there together with three of the local councillors. They will be pleased to explain the development plans in more detail.

If you should have any comments, there will be feedback forms on the table at the back of the room.

An open meeting will be held at the end of July to discuss these plans. These plans with any changes will then be submitted in August for approval by the local authority.

<u>Organic Farm Foods</u>

A second store of Organic Farm Foods will open shortly in the centre of Ipswich. Its aim is to employ up to 15 people from the local community. Training will be given to the successful job seekers.

All profits will be put back into the company. Most of the food products for sale will be organic. Produce that is ethically grown will also be sold.

The branch will be open from 10 am to 4 pm Monday to Saturday. Cars can be parked at the rear of the store. There will also be a coffee shop. This will sell fairtrade coffee and tea as well as snacks.

Please visit us soon.

EXERCISE AT 1.10: WORKED EXAMPLE

DOCUMENT 3

PROFESSIONAL CONDUCT

Looking for a job in the current climate is very competitive. If you want to land that perfect job there cannot be any mistakes. With strong competition in the job market you need to present yourself to the best of your ability.

Flexible working hours are now normal practice. However, you should not forget that every member of staff must adhere to work rules. For instance some firms may not accept you surfing the internet or making private phone calls during office hours. Others may turn a blind eye towards it.

There is a legal duty for employers to check your identity. Something that is untrue on your

CV will damage your employment record. False qualifications and misleading claims could

lose you a job offer.

With references, ask your most recent or past employer if they will be able to help you. **Always assume that your CV or job application form will be fully checked.**

Do not risk harming your employment record by deceit.

EXERCISE AT 1.11: WORKED EXAMPLE

DOCUMENT 3

ENERGY SAVINGS

Many people are now looking for ways in which they can save money.

The installation of solar panels is now very popular. Using the rays of the sun to heat tubes placed on the roof of a building will provide enough hot water for a family. These panels will operate effectively for many years.   Even on the cloudiest of days the panels will provide you with a constant supply of hot water.

Although the outlay seems costly, the savings will soon show in your heating bills.

Our system can be fitted to a standard or combination boiler. A separate storage tank will need

to be fitted for the combination system. These tanks are already lagged before being fitted. The

installation of the panels is fairly easy. Expert fitters are used for each aspect of the job. There

will be no damage to your property either internally or externally.

Access is required to the loft to secure the solar panels and connect the necessary pipe work.

EXERCISE AT 1.12: WORKED EXAMPLE

PROGRESS FRIENDLY SOCIETY

This report aims to give members a short summary of our achievements over the past year.

Throughout the year we were able to sustain a high level of service to all our members.

One example was during the recent flash flooding. Our claims team straight away telephoned all our clients living in the affected regions. Advice and help with making a claim was given. **As a result claims were paid out within a week.**

As you will no doubt be aware, our support helpline is open throughout the day and night. During the year we were able to assist a number of members and their families in financial hardship. Our support fund was set up just to deal with such cases.

Towards the end of the year our members took part in a survey. We were delighted that over 90% were satisfied with the service they received. In addition most of these said they would purchase more products from us in the future.

EXAM AT 1.A1: WORKED EXAMPLE

DOCUMENT 1

Plaudit Credit Reference Agency
Robin Hood Mews
NOTTINGHAM
NG23 8FT

Telephone: 01522 990033
Email: plaudit@cra.co.uk

Our ref MA/WTP

3 March 2010

Mr Gerwyn Rees
22 Forest Avenue
Burton Joyce
NOTTINGHAM
NG14 7CR

Dear Mr Rees

CREDIT REPORT

Thank you for your application for a credit report. The report includes all the details that we hold about you. This information has been sent from companies with which you have had financial dealings.

I enclose a leaflet explaining the different types of data that may be included. The leaflet should answer any queries you may have. It also explains the steps you should take if you have any questions. If there are problems with the details companies have submitted you will need to make direct contact with them. Their consent will be required before any changes can be made.

Your credit report has been revised to include other names by which you have been known. It also includes links to former addresses. If this information is incorrect and needs to be changed please contact us.

Yours sincerely

Millie Ashleigh
Consumer Help Service

Enc

EXAM AT 1.A2: WORKED EXAMPLE

DOCUMENT 2

MEMORANDUM

To:	Takashi Kondo, Building Inspector
From:	Lloyd Evans, Surveyor and Valuator
Ref:	LE/TK
Date:	3 March 2010

<u>5 Albany Crescent Bournemouth</u>

I carried out a survey on the above property today. This was to locate the cause of the damp and suggest any remedial work. The weather was dry following a very wet spell.

I have not inspected covered or inaccessible areas. Neither have I included parts that are in good order or repair. The report should not be taken as making any implied statement about such parts.

I have not carried out any searches into past or present use of the property.

I will forward a detailed report to you as soon as it is ready together with a valuation.

EXAM AT 1.A3: WORKED EXAMPLE

DOCUMENT 3

FIRE SAFETY REPORT FOR ARENA LEISURE CENTRE

This report provides a review of the risk to life from fire in this building. Recommendations are to ensure fire safety orders are met.

The building appears secure and arrangements are made for storage and disposal of waste. The main staircase provides the only means of escape. It is vital the staircase is not blocked and should remain a safe area. Emergency lighting is working within the centre.

Faulty electrical equipment is a major cause of fire. It is necessary that measures are taken to ensure all equipment is in good working order. All portable appliances should be PAT tested and kept up to date.

Smoking is prohibited throughout the building. No smoking signs should be placed in all areas of the centre. Fire safety signs and notices are good. A sign should be displayed by the lift stating it must not be used in the event of fire.

All testing should be recorded in the Fire Safety Log Book.

EXAM AT 1.B1: WORKED EXAMPLE

DOCUMENT1

Progress Group
Westwood Way
COVENTRY
CV4 8JQ

024 7647 0033

3 March 2010

Our ref CD/LA

Mr and Mrs John Flanagan
29 The Meadows
DONCASTER
DN1 7DW

Dear Mr and Mrs Flanagan

ENGLISH ROSE CRUISE HOLIDAY

I was sorry to receive your letter of complaint about your recent cruise holiday on our ship English Rose. I have noted all of your problems some of which I had already been told about. You can be assured that a full investigation will be carried out.

I have found out that you were given the wrong cabin. You were shown to a lower deck cabin when you should have had an upper deck cabin. This error was not discovered until another couple boarded the liner at Gibraltar. By this time you were settled. You did not wish to move for the rest of your cruise.

I am enclosing a cheque in full compensation for the difference in the cost of your accommodation.

Once my investigations have been completed I will contact you again

Yours faithfully

Carol Domanski
General Manager

Enc

DOCUMENT 2

MEMORANDUM

To   Gwyn Evans

From   Eileen Yeo

Date   3 March 2010

Ref   EY/RH

Open Evenings

The classes in our new building will start from September. We are holding a series of open evenings next week. All managers will be attending.

I am looking for volunteers from the teaching staff to attend at least one night. A voucher for an evening meal and drink will be given to each member of staff who is on duty. There will also be an amount of four hours to be placed on your holiday record for future time off.

All managers have prepared superb presentations to market the new courses. I hope you will come along and provide the extra support required to promote these courses.

EXAM AT 1.B3: WORKED EXAMPLE

DOCUMENT 3

REPORT ON STRUCTURAL PROBLEMS

The surveyor has now completed his investigations.

There appears to be a large area on the ground floor that is very damp. The wall near the door is very wet. This could be caused by a blocked gutter and down pipe on the outside of the building. The timber is rotting and the wallpaper is peeling off. On the opposite side the wall is damp with some dry rot in the wood. The moisture level in the floor is above the acceptable level. A waterproof coating will be required before the floor covering is laid.

The front door is poorly fitted. This is due to the excessive moisture on the front right hand side

of the framework.

The restoration work in the kitchen has exposed a fireplace complete with dog grate and old ash. **This should be cleaned out and boarded up.**

All of the ceiling tiles are worn and cracked. These tiles will need to be replaced as they are beyond renovation.

Progress Group
180 Leopold Road
MULBARTON
Norfolk
NR14 9HZ

01508 777656

Our ref DR/WK

3 March 2010

Mrs Sharon Wood
168 Hellesdon Drive
LITTLE PLUMSTEAD
Norfolk
NR13 4LT

Dear Mrs Wood

INTEREST RATES

We would like to thank you for saving with our bank.

A leaflet showing the current interest rates on your two savings accounts is enclosed. In addition details of our other accounts are listed. You will therefore be able to see whether you are getting the best return on your money. If not, it is possible for you to transfer your savings to another account.

You may also like to know about our individual savings account. This is free of income tax. It also gives a very good rate of interest which is paid annually. Money can be paid in either in a lump sum or each month by direct debit.

Our staff will be only too pleased to give advice on any of these matters. Please telephone us during office hours for an appointment.

Yours sincerely

Donald Redfern
Director of Savings

Enc

EXAM AT 1.C2: WORKED EXAMPLE

<u>Smith and Brown Insurance</u>

This is to inform our loyal clients that Smith and Brown Insurance is to close its office in Church Street. This is because of major structural faults within the building. All tenants have been asked to move out by the end of this month. The renovation will take about three months.

We are pleased to announce that we will be moving to an office next to the library. This will be a temporary measure only. We do hope all our clients will understand the situation. We do not expect this to affect our daily business in any way.

We look forward to your continued support over this rather unsettling period of time.

FASTER PAYMENTS

At its meeting last month group members agreed to see if the transfer of funds could be made more efficient. A special committee was set up to look into this. As a result a service called Faster Payments is being offered. This will come into effect at the end of next month.

It will give customers a faster way of transferring money from one account to another. **In most cases this means that funds will be received on the same working day.** Not all banks offer this faster service so customers should go online for further details.

The Faster Payments plan only allows for amounts of up to £10,000 to be transferred. Once a payment has been made it cannot be cancelled. The charge for each transfer is £5.

The introduction of this plan means that there will be changes to our terms and conditions.

We feel sure that all our customers will benefit from this new scheme. Please contact us if you have any queries.